Looking

FOR

Christmas

DONNA VANLIERE

HARVEST HOUSE PUBLISHERS
EUGENE, OREGON

Unless otherwise indicated, all Scripture verses are taken from the *Holy Bible*, New Living Translation, copyright © 1996, 2004, 2015 by Tyndale House Foundation. Used with permission of Tyndale House Publishers, Inc., Carol Stream, Illinois 60188. All rights reserved.

Other Bible translations used are credited in the back of the book.

Cover design by Faceout Studio, Addie Lutzo
Cover images created by Addie Lutzo / Faceout Studio
Interior design by Janelle Coury
Interior images © Yuliia_Pizhivska, In Art, pingebat, lukbar, Inkingman Esfir se / Shutterstock

For bulk, special sales, or ministry purchases, please call 1-800-547-8979.
Email: CustomerService@hhpbooks.com

This logo is a federally registered trademark of the Hawkins Children's LLC. Harvest House Publishers, Inc., is the exclusive licensee of this trademark.

LOOKING FOR CHRISTMAS

Copyright © 2025 by Donna VanLiere
Published by Harvest House Publishers
Eugene, Oregon 97408
www.harvesthousepublishers.com

ISBN 978-0-7369-9211-4 (hardcover)
ISBN 978-0-7369-9212-1 (eBook)

Library of Congress Control Number: 2024951616

Printed in China

25 26 27 28 29 30 31 32 33 / DC / 10 9 8 7 6 5 4 3 2 1

FOR PEGGY RIXSON,
WHO WAS ONE OF MY EARLIEST
CHILDHOOD FRIENDS,
AND WHO IS STILL A FRIEND TODAY.

Acknowledgment

Excerpts from THE CHRISTMAS JOURNEY by Donna VanLiere. Copyright © 2010 by Donna VanLiere. Used by permission of St. Martin's Publishing Group. All Rights Reserved.

Contents

The Charlie Brown in All of Us

You remember the scene from the 1965 television special *A Charlie Brown Christmas*: Charlie Brown is confiding in his pal Linus on a bright, wintry day but something is amiss. Charlie Brown tells his friend that something must be wrong with him because even though Christmas is coming, he's just not happy. He's not feeling the way he's "supposed to feel." He chalks it up that he simply doesn't understand Christmas. Sure, he likes getting presents and sending Christmas cards and decorating trees, but he's still not happy. As a matter of fact, he feels downright depressed.

Apparently, Charlie Brown had been watching too many Christmas commercials and movies, where idyllic decorations brighten every corner of a home and attractive, good-natured family members laugh easily with one another while pajama-clad children chatter like Santa's elves over board games and puzzles in front of a large, roaring fire. In our imaginations, we envision our friends and coworkers with a beautiful tree, a delicious meal, and shiny, happy faces, enjoying it all. Christmas is, after all, for two-car, two-career families in towns called Pleasantville. Somehow we, along with Charlie Brown, have been sold a bill of goods saying that's what Christmas is all about.

Where did it all go south, and how did we get it so wrong? While picture-perfect, happy people enjoy the presents and the feast of Christmas, that's not how it all began. Jesus was not born in a mansion or castle or surrounded by nobility. He was born to a simple peasant woman and her carpenter husband so that He could sympathize with our brokenness, heartache, pain, and disappointments. The first people who took the time to find Him were not kings or queens or celebrities of any kind. They were shepherds who were working the night shift.

"Do not be afraid," the angel said to them. "I bring you good news of great joy." Perhaps the shepherds were thinking weekends off with pay, but the angel went on. "Today in the town of David a Savior has been born to you; he is Christ the Lord."

A Savior has come for the girl who left home at 16 and for the father who drove her away. A Rescuer has come for every child who has been abandoned by a parent. A Healer has come to bind up the wounds of the one who can't escape the trauma of childhood. A Redeemer has come for every man or woman whose train wreck of a life careened off the rails years ago. They're among the ones Christmas is for!

Christmas is for the lonely and the brokenhearted. It's for the widow or the family with an empty chair around their table. It's for the single mom who works two jobs to feed her kids. It's for the young woman who works in strip clubs and the mother at home who worries about her. Christmas is for the homeless man who waits for the doors of the rescue mission to open for a hot meal and for the lonely millionaire tucked away behind the moat that is his front yard.

Christmas is for everyone who keeps looking for love in all the wrong places and hoping deep in their hearts that the hope of the Nativity really does exist. Christmas is for those who have lost everything: their job, their fortune, their good name, their family, or their dreams. Christmas is for those who punch a time clock and have swollen feet. It's for those who ride a train an hour and a half each way for work and for those who sell beauty and glamour when they themselves feel ugly and lost.

Christ came down from heaven to heal broken marriages and mend fractured families. He came for those who drink too much, smoke like chimneys, inhale from a crack pipe, sell their bodies, or are addicted to online shopping, power, status, cosmetic procedures, work, exercise, money, or food. He came for those who find their happiness in a pill bottle, for those who gamble away everything, and for those who hide a burner phone from their spouse. He came for the depressed, the lonely, the anxious, the stressed, the hopeless, and the discouraged.

That dark, smelly Nativity scene filled with the stink and noise of animals is not a place to look down on or be pitied, but rather, it was the beginning of hope for us all. Grace was born there. Peace penetrated our hopelessness there. Love shone bright in our darkness there. That is our comfort and joy.

Like Charlie Brown, if Christmas has got you down, if you can't find Christ in Christmas, if you're feeling that your life somehow doesn't measure up to the hype, then the truth of the Nativity is for you!

Like the shepherds, let's go to Bethlehem and look for the manger. Let's explore why the birth of Jesus in that stable more than 2,000 years ago is the dividing point of history. Like Mary, let's treasure all these things, pondering them in our hearts. And like the magi, let's go on a journey to worship the King of kings!

ONE

Looking at Mary

I AM THE LORD'S SERVANT. MAY EVERYTHING YOU HAVE SAID ABOUT ME COME TRUE (LUKE 1:38).

*J*oseph's stomach rumbles as he packs the donkey. He should have eaten more but is anxious to get on the road. His eyes meet Mary's as he helps her onto the donkey. He nods and she smiles in the half-light. Joseph walks beside the donkey, and although he does not look at them, he feels the eyes of his neighbors as they pass. The chattering of three women drawing water ceases as he and Mary go by, and Mary keeps her head down. She has long known what they think of her. The laughter of two men mending a fishing net subsides to a whisper as the donkey approaches, and children stop playing in the street when their mothers clack their tongues and snap their fingers.

Joseph sets his jaw and ignores them, relieved to get away for a while. Angels of God had visited him and Mary about this baby, but they hadn't visited everyone in town. Joseph has heard the townspeople ridicule Mary. He has seen them point and then turn away, ostracizing her with *their clenched teeth and cold shoulders. "Perversion," they have said. "Prostituted under the nose of her father." The gossiped indictments and whispered innuendoes have seeped under every doorway. The conception was not cloaked in anonymity. Everyone knew her name. They knew her father and mother's names. Joseph's own heart has throbbed with a dull pain for weeks, and looking at Mary, he wonders how someone so young is able to bear the burden of such a stigma.*

Mary lays her hands on her swollen belly. The baby dropped into the birth canal days ago, causing increasing discomfort. A chill clings to the shadows that stretch over the sleepy town, and Joseph places a thin blanket over Mary's legs. The morning echoes grow distant as they thread their way out of town, and Joseph's tensions ease.

"Are you well?" he asks.

"I am," she says, smiling, rubbing her stomach. "He is no longer stirring but is heavy inside."[1]

I wrote that years ago for a book called *The Christmas Journey* to illustrate what Joseph and Mary might have endured when the townspeople of the sleepy village of Nazareth learned that she was pregnant before marriage. The Bible says that Mary was "confused and disturbed" by what the angel Gabriel had said to her (Luke 1:29). Gabriel saw her reaction and told her not to be afraid because she had found favor with God. The thoughts that must have been swirling in her mind! She was not royalty; she was unknown, a nobody and nothing special. Her family was part and parcel of the peasant people in Nazareth, a completely undistinguished town. In this little backwater hamlet, how in the world had she found favor with God?

Gabriel wasn't finished. He went on, "You will conceive and give birth to a son, and you will name him Jesus. He will be very great and will be called the Son of the Most High. The Lord God will give him the throne of his ancestor David. And he will reign over Israel forever; his Kingdom will never end!" (verses 31-33).

At this point, Mary must have been trying to catch her breath, her thoughts spinning. She, little Mary from Nazareth, would give birth to a son who would sit on the throne of David? He would reign over Israel forever? His kingdom would never end? Kings didn't come from Nazareth! And that was just the smallest bit of the confusion she felt.

Mary found her voice. Mystified and bewildered, she asked, "How can this happen? I am a virgin" (verse 34).

Gabriel explained how it would happen, and we can only imagine what it must have been like from his perspective to see her face! "The Holy Spirit will come upon you, and the power of the Most High will overshadow you. So the baby to be born will be holy, and he will be called the Son of God. What's more, your relative Elizabeth has become pregnant in her old age! People used to say she was barren, but she has conceived a son and is now in her sixth month. For the word of God will never fail" (verses 35-37).

She, a virgin, would carry the Son of God. But the miracles did not stop there. Her cousin Elizabeth, who was very old, would also give birth to a son! After centuries of silence, during which God had not spoken through His prophets or an angel of the Lord, God's own Son would be stepping down into their world to be with them. God would no longer be silent! This would be too much for anyone to process, let alone a young teenager about to be married. Surely, Mary's heart was thumping inside her chest. But instead of being scared and focused on herself, Mary put her trust in the Lord and said, "I am the Lord's servant. May everything you have said about me come true. And then the angel left her" (verse 38).

Mary knew that being pregnant without being married meant she could be stoned to death. She knew it meant she would be the buzz of gossip in her little village. She knew that she would live with scorn and rejection from those around her. At that point, she did not know the joy and sorrow that the baby forming inside her would bring to her. She did not know that she would not die in obscurity like the other women in her village, but that she would be honored for centuries to come. She did not know that she would carry the child who would make each of us a child of God.

Mary couldn't comprehend that she would feed bread to the Bread of Life or help the One dress who would robe her in righteousness. She could not foresee that the tiny hands that would wrap around her fingers as He learned to walk would open the eyes of the blind and heal the diseased and one day be nailed to a Roman cross. She couldn't grasp that within her womb a little mouth would form that had spoken the world into existence and would grow up to speak the very Word of God. She couldn't fathom the baby's feet that would kick from inside her womb would someday walk up Calvary's hill to His own execution.

She couldn't see what was ahead and didn't have all the answers. But she said yes to God anyway.

GOD'S FAVOR

Gabriel called Mary "favored woman" (Luke 1:28), and the biblical meaning is that she was imbued with special honor. Of all the women on the earth, she was given the privilege of carrying God's Son (and she would receive Him as her Savior, just like all others who believe), but Gabriel didn't say she was perfect or sinless. "For all have sinned and fall short of the glory of God" (Romans 3:23 NKJV). "All" in that verse means all. It doesn't exclude anyone. Mary was a sinner, just like you and I are sinners, but God had chosen her. The Bible doesn't say why she was chosen except that she was a virgin; the other reasons are known only by God alone. But we do know these things about Mary from Scripture:

+ We know that she was a woman of faith because she believed the Lord would do what He said.

+ We know she praised the Lord and magnified His name.

+ We know she was in awe of the Lord and recognized His mercies.

+ We know she recognized God's power to scatter the proud and lift up the humble.

+ We know she was hungry for the good things of God.

+ We know she felt God's love and mercy for Israel because she knew that God keeps His promises.

+ We know she knew God's Word because nearly all the words from her prayer in Luke 1:46-55 are from Scripture.

+ And we know she was obedient because she put her yes on the table when she said to Gabriel, "I am the Lord's servant. May everything you have said about me come true" (Luke 1:38).

For a common and ordinary girl living in a plain, ordinary village where nothing ever changed, the birth of God's Son would ricochet around the world, and nothing would ever be the same again.

MARY'S RESPONSE

+ The angel Gabriel told Mary that she was pregnant, but humanly speaking, that was impossible—she was a virgin. Gabriel said to her, "The Holy Spirit will come upon you, and the power of the Most High will overshadow you" (Luke 1:35). God's answer to Mary's confusion was the Holy Spirit. His answer to the impossible in her life was the Holy Spirit. What God was about to accomplish could not be done by human means, but only by divine power. And when we ask Jesus to be Lord and Savior of our lives, the Holy Spirit takes up residence inside us so that He can give us the power and strength needed for each impossible circumstance in our lives. " 'You will not succeed by your own strength or by your own power, but by my Spirit,' says the LORD All-Powerful" (Zechariah 4:6 NCV). It is the Holy Spirit's power that guides and leads us through dark valleys and deep waters.

✦ The next words out of Mary's mouth didn't begin with "but." She didn't say, "But I'll be shunned because I'll be pregnant and unmarried," or "But this will bring shame on my family." She responded in submission by saying, "I am the Lord's servant. May everything you have said about me come true" (Luke 1:38). She wasn't delusional or denying her circumstances. She was simply aligning her words with God's promise. Words matter. We use them every day in conversations, emails, texts, letters, or social media posts. It's our choice how we use them. "The tongue can bring death or life" (Proverbs 18:21). Mary could have used her words to argue and put up a fight, but that would have brought turmoil and difficulty into the situation. She chose to use her words to confirm that she believed God's word and was stepping out in faith.

✦ Mary then did a wise thing. The Bible doesn't tell us if it was her idea or if she was encouraged by her parents, but she went to visit her cousin Elizabeth, who was also supernaturally pregnant. Mary chose to spend time with her elderly cousin, who, by biology alone, should not have been pregnant...but God! For three months, Mary surrounded herself with people who also believed God's word in impossible circumstances. Who we choose to be with impacts our faith and life choices. Mary was with people who believed God's promises despite what reality looked like and she was in a home where her faith would grow. If we want to experience abiding joy and peace, we need to surround ourselves with those who will help our faith in Jesus to grow, and cause our trust in God's Word to become deeper.

When Elizabeth heard Mary's greeting, the baby within her jumped for joy and Elizabeth was filled with the Holy Spirit. As he was being formed in his mother's womb, Elizabeth's unborn child was the first to recognize and respond to Jesus. And at the very moment that her baby jumped, Elizabeth was filled with the Holy Spirit! She said to Mary, "You are blessed because you believed that the Lord would do what he said" (Luke 1:45). Mary hadn't told Elizabeth she was pregnant. She hadn't said anything beyond a greeting—it was the Holy Spirit within Elizabeth who revealed this information to her. After that, Mary couldn't help but begin praising the Lord.

Oh, how my soul praises the Lord.
How my spirit rejoices in God my Savior!
For he took notice of his lowly servant girl,
    and from now on all generations will
      call me blessed.
For the Mighty One is holy,
    and he has done great things for me
                (verses 46-49).

✦ Mary was praising and giving God the glory even before the promised birth of Jesus! She had no comprehension of the heartache, difficulties, or challenges that were ahead, but that wasn't her focus. Her song of praise was about God's faithfulness, His mercies, and His fulfilled promises. We can't linger on the "What ifs…?" in our present situation or future circumstances. Like Mary, we must focus on God's faithfulness, His goodness, His kindness, His grace, His mercies, and His fulfilled promises to us. When we do that, we can't help but praise the Lord!

Mary was favored by God. Throughout her life, she may have questioned why she was chosen and most certainly would have remembered words from the Scriptures, particularly the prophet Isaiah, who said, "The Lord himself will give you the sign. Look! The virgin will conceive a child! She will give birth to a son and will call him Immanuel (which means 'God is with us')"(Isaiah

7:14). Quickly thereafter, Mary would have recalled the angel Gabriel's words to her: "The word of God will never fail" (Luke 1:37). Indeed, God's word had never failed.

Mary honored her word and provided a loving home for God's only Son. She laughed and cried as she raised Jesus through His childhood and stood weeping in anguish as Romans raised Him up on a cross. She was the only one who had been present with Jesus from the cradle to the cross. And through everything, the Lord was with her. Just as He is with you.

TWO

Looking at Mary's Hometown

NAZARETH!...CAN ANYTHING GOOD COME
FROM NAZARETH? (JOHN 1:46).

he village of Nazareth was situated in a remote and unremarkable corner of Galilee. No one bragged about being from there. The town had no prestigious acclaim for religion or education. No one was vacationing there or competing for a home to buy. Rome kept a regional garrison there, so most Jewish people viewed the area as unclean. When Philip told Nathanael that Jesus of Nazareth, the very person whom Moses had written about, had been found, Nathanael scoffed, saying, "Nazareth!…Can anything good come from Nazareth?" (John 1:46). That pretty much summed up what people thought of the town.

Nothing exciting happened in the little village. Nothing except the ordinary, and only the common and ordinary lived there, like Mary and her family. Mary's days would have been filled by grinding grain, helping her mother cook, fetching water from the well, watching over younger siblings, sewing and mending, and helping to keep the home tidy. But amid the mundane, her thoughts must have turned to her upcoming wedding to Joseph. In the first century, the focus of the wedding was on the man, unlike the way our culture focuses on the bride. Once the man was finished building an extra room onto his father's home, it was the father who would tell his son to go get his bride and bring her home. The young woman never knew when the man would be coming for her; she had to be ready day or night for his arrival.

THE BETROTHAL

There is no record of how old Mary was, but if we look at the time and culture in which she lived, we can assume she was a teenager. According to rabbinic texts, parents arranged the marriages of their children and girls were engaged at around age 12, about the time of puberty, and would marry a year later. First-century archaeological evidence exists that lists women's age-of-marriage generally between 12 to 17 years, with the majority at age 13.[2] Mary's parents had arranged her marriage to Joseph, a carpenter, who was probably around the same age or possibly a few years older.

Joseph and Mary were betrothed to one another.

According to Jewish custom at this time, betrothal was a form of engagement; the marriage vows were spoken at the betrothal, which made it more binding than what we call engagement today and could only be broken by divorce.[3] Joseph and Mary had not yet had an official ceremony in which they were married in front of family and friends. That, and the celebration to follow, would come later.

Due to the size of Nazareth, Mary and Joseph may have known each other from childhood. Their upcoming marriage would not only unite them, but both of their families as well. In the monotony of her everyday life, we can imagine the dreams that stirred in Mary's mind and the excitement she felt in her heart about becoming Joseph's wife.

THE ANNOUNCEMENT THAT CHANGED EVERYTHING

We don't know where Mary was or what time of day it happened, but on an ordinary day in that ordinary village, the extraordinary happened.

The angel Gabriel appeared before her. This is the same Gabriel who stands in the presence of God (Luke 1:19) and who explained a vision to Daniel approximately 600 years earlier. Six months before appearing to Mary, he also announced to Zechariah the priest (Mary's cousin Elizabeth's husband) that they would have a son (Luke 1:13).

Gabriel said to Mary, "Greetings, favored woman! The Lord is with you!" (Luke 1:28).

As mentioned earlier, Mary lived at the time when the Lord had fallen silent. About 400 years of silence went by, without any prophets hearing a word from the Lord—400 years! By this time, the Romans had conquered Judea, which left the inhabitants uneasy and oftentimes angry. Where was the word of the Lord in any of this? Why hadn't God communicated with His people? The Bible doesn't say, but in the last book of the Old Testament (the New Testament opens 400 years later), the prophet Malachi said,

> You have wearied the LORD with your words.
>
> "How have we wearied him?" you ask.
>
> You have wearied him by saying that all who do evil are good in the LORD's sight, and he is pleased with them. You have wearied him by asking, "Where is the God of justice?" (Malachi 2:17).

Throughout the previous centuries, God had open dialogue with His people. He would tell them how to walk with Him and how He would bless them. The Israelites would obey for a time, but then they would

worship false gods and fall into open rebellion and disobedience. This cycle of obedience to rebellion happened again and again, and now in Malachi, the people
are basically saying that God is the problem, not them.
"How have *we* wearied him?"

God's words were not getting through to them.
Maybe that is why four centuries of silence followed the
end of the Old Testament. But then Malachi closed on
a remarkable note:

> Look, I am sending you the prophet Elijah
> before the great and dreadful day of the LORD
> arrives. His preaching will turn the hearts of
> fathers to their children, and the hearts of chil-
> dren to their fathers (Malachi 4:5).

There would be another Elijah who would mend
families and turn people to the Lord! For the next
400 years, the Jews who were faithful held on to this
promise. Now Gabriel was standing in front of Mary,
delivering a word from the Lord. This must have been
overwhelming for her! Surely this meant that all of Israel
would soon hear more from God again. Mary had little
concept of what God had in store for her and the world.
She didn't realize that the joy of Christmas would soon
be in reach for all of us.

THREE

Looking at Joseph

Mary watches the donkey drink. "Are you frightened, Joseph?" she asks.

He looks up at her. Every illusion he had of starting a family with her ended months ago when she told him she was pregnant. Every conceivable dream of the village celebrating their wedding shattered when rumor swelled that his betrothed was a harlot. Swept away with those dreams were his plans and desires and every expectation that he had for their new life together. He was torn from the privacy of a once-quiet life and shifted into one of public shame and ridicule.

He is still trying to wrap his mind around all that has taken place in so short a time. He watches Mary as the corners of her mouth turn up in soft edges. For months now, those she has grown up with, who have shared meals around her family's table, have been quick to brand her, but these well-mannered guardians of morality never even cupped their ear to hear the truth or offered a word of compassion. The hourglass has been turned and eternity is fast approaching, but their thoughts have been consumed with how the law of Moses is unwavering concerning what to do with those caught in sexual sin. The very angel who came to Mary all those months ago must surely have guarded her life from the hatred and condemnation of the righteous bent on vengeance in the name of God. How else has her life been spared? Is she frightened? He cannot tell. He hasn't known her long enough to discern her emotions or fears. They are both so new to each other.

"The angel told me not to be afraid," he says. He breaks the bread in two and hands her a piece. "I wish I could say that I am not, but I am. I am terrified." He watches as others gather around the well. "What does that make me?"

She sits on the ground and reaches for a fig. "As human as I," she says.[4]

A SENSITIVE AND HUMBLE MAN

Dreams had long been important in Israel. Even today, many people pay attention to their dreams because they often are used by God to bring a warning, a promise, encouragement, or convey what will happen now or in the future. Joseph worked as a carpenter and was probably a simple, levelheaded, orderly, and practical man. His skills, like any carpenter at that time, lay in precise measurement (measure twice, cut once), seeing the job complete in his mind before it was started, knowledge of the characteristics of wood and which to use for a particular project, and keeping his workplace safe (in the first century, a simple cut could quickly turn into an infection and end a life). As a carpenter, Joseph would have worked on anything from home construction to furniture building and crafting tools.

Like Mary, in the routine of his day, while measuring, sawing, and building, Joseph must have been looking ahead to his wedding day and his life with Mary. Perhaps he even dreamed of teaching his sons his craft. It was hard work, but he knew that it would provide for their families, just as he knew he would be able to provide for Mary and their family together.

As a carpenter, Joseph undoubtedly knew most everyone in the village because his skill would be in high demand. So imagine his disbelief when he discovered that Mary was pregnant. The feelings of anger, betrayal, hurt, fear, and revenge must have swept over him in waves. How could Mary do this? She seemed as happy as he was about their upcoming marriage. Everyone in Nazareth would be talking about this! Who was the father? Did he simply use her and then run off? The

Bible doesn't tell us whether Mary shared the news of her pregnancy with him or if he saw the baby bump developing. It says, "Joseph, to whom she was engaged, was a righteous man and did not want to disgrace her publicly, so he decided to break the engagement quietly" (Matthew 1:19).

As I mentioned earlier, Joseph and Mary were betrothed, which was more binding than a typical engagement. They had said some vows to one another, but that was not the actual wedding ceremony. Jewish custom stipulated that the couple did not live together or consummate their union until after the ceremony, and any unfaithfulness by the betrothed was treated as adultery and was punishable by death, according to Jewish law.[5]

Joseph knew the law and that Mary could be stoned to death for being pregnant outside of marriage. Whatever feelings he may have initially felt when he discovered that Mary was pregnant were soon overshadowed by the love he felt for her. Because he was a good and righteous man, Joseph decided to break their engagement quietly so that she would not suffer any public disgrace. What a gracious response in the face of what anyone would count as a betrayal! Joseph was not thinking of himself at this moment (the law would have been on his side), but he was thinking of Mary and the baby.

This was not the act of a proud and vindictive man, but rather, of a sensitive, loving, and humble man.

THE DREAMS

Obviously, Joseph did not make his decision known right away, but rather, "slept on it."

> As he considered this, an angel of the Lord appeared to him in a dream. "Joseph, son of David," the angel said, "do not be afraid to take Mary as your wife. For the child within her was conceived by the Holy Spirit. And she will have a son, and you are to name him Jesus, for he will save his people from their sins."
>
> All of this occurred to fulfill the Lord's message through his prophet:
>
> > "Look! The virgin will conceive a child!
> >   She will give birth to a son,
> > and they will call him Immanuel,
> >   which means 'God is with us'"
> >   (Matthew 1:20-23).

An unnamed angel appears in Joseph's dream and explains what has happened. It's interesting that an angel did not visit Joseph in person like Gabriel did with Mary, but rather, appeared to him in a dream. Why? Perhaps because God reaches each of us in ways that we can understand. For Joseph, a pragmatic man who worked with his hands, an in-person visit from an angel might have proved to be too much to handle. But a dream in which an angel explained the situation and told him what to do was a different matter. Again, dreams were important throughout the history of the Jews.

Being a faithful man who attended synagogue, Joseph would know the scripture that the angel had quoted from the prophet Isaiah. Mary, *his* Mary, was the virgin mentioned in that ancient text, and he would be Jesus' earthly father. How would any man process that? It is an inconceivable thought. The time of silence was now over; God would be with them in the flesh. We can't begin to comprehend what Joseph might have been thinking. But we do know that "when Joseph woke up, he did as the angel of the Lord commanded and took Mary as his wife" (verse 24).

Joseph could have woken up and doubted what he had dreamed. He still could have walked away, but he didn't. At that moment, he chose to believe that what the angel had said in the dream was true and chose to be Jesus' adoptive father. He chose to trust God with his life and Mary's, and the life of the child she carried. He didn't announce this to all of Nazareth, but he got out of bed and walked forward in simple obedience and faith. Through just a few sentences in the Nativity narrative, we can see why God chose Joseph to be the earthly father of Jesus. From the Old Testament prophecies, Joseph knew that what was about to take place was not about him or even Mary; it was all about Jesus, the long-awaited Messiah. Another man may have tried to worm his way into the spotlight, but not Joseph. That was not his way. He was a quiet, dependable, behind-the-scenes man.

✦ Other dreams would guide Joseph in the years ahead. While still in Bethlehem with Mary and Jesus, we read of Joseph's second dream: "After the wise men were gone, an angel of the Lord *appeared to Joseph in a dream.* 'Get up! Flee to Egypt with the child and his mother,' the angel said. 'Stay there until I tell you to return, because Herod is going to search for the child to kill him'" (Matthew 2:13). Again, with faith and obedience Joseph did as he was warned, fulfilling the prophecy in Hosea 11:1 that God's beloved son would be called out of Egypt.

✦ While in Egypt, Joseph had a third dream:

When Herod died, an angel of the Lord appeared in a dream to Joseph in Egypt. "Get up!" the angel said. "Take the child and his mother back to the land of Israel, because those who were trying to kill the child are dead." So Joseph got up and returned to the land of Israel with Jesus and his mother (Matthew 2:19-21).

While the young family was in Egypt, Herod died. With this assurance that those who wanted to kill Jesus were now dead, Joseph packed up Mary and Jesus and went back to Canaan, or the land of Israel.

✦ Yet in the very next verse we read about Joseph's fourth and final dream: "When he learned that the new ruler of Judea was Herod's son Archelaus, he was afraid to go there. Then, after being warned in a dream, he left for the region of Galilee. So the family went and lived in a town called Nazareth. This fulfilled what the prophets had said: 'He will be called a Nazarene'" (Matthew 2:22-23). Mary and Joseph were now back where they started—in Nazareth.

In each of these dreams, we see not only Joseph's faith, obedience, and unwavering trust in God, but we see what a great protector he was for his family. Each time he was warned of danger, he immediately jumped into action to protect them. Jesus may not have been Joseph's flesh and blood, but Joseph loved, cared for, and protected Him as if He were because in God's love, the bonds of adoption are just as strong as flesh and blood. As a mother of three adopted children, I can unequivocally say that there is no difference.

A GOOD AND FAITHFUL MAN

"How will I teach him?"

"How do you teach any child?" she asks.

He turns his face to her. "Yes. But how do you teach him?" They eat in silence as the question fills the air around them. "How will I raise him?"

"With love," she says.

He looks at her. "But is love from a common man enough?"

She traces her finger through the blades of grass in front of her. "It will be more than enough," she says. "It is the very reason he's coming."[6]

There was no parenting book on how to train up the future King of kings, so Joseph would father Jesus in the way he knew how: with faith, consistency, and simplicity. He would teach Jesus how to work with His hands and take Him to synagogue. He would wrap his arm around Him when he was proud of the fine work He had done helping him in the carpenter shop that day. He would remind Jesus to look after His mother and to honor her. When people in the village looked at Joseph, they probably viewed him as a good and righteous man and a wonderful father.

Many believe the reason Joseph is not mentioned alongside Mary in Bible narratives beyond the time that Jesus was 12 is probably because Joseph had died. The fact is that it was commonplace for people to die at a young age in the first century. Joseph very well may have been in his early or late thirties when he died, giving him plenty of time to father several children (if he was 18 at the time of Jesus' birth, he would have been 30 when Jesus was 12 and Joseph was last mentioned). The Bible tells us that Jesus was Mary's firstborn son (Luke 2:7), meaning there would be others. Scripture records four brothers and some sisters:

> He's just the carpenter's son, and we know Mary, his mother, and his brothers—James, Joseph, Simon, and Judas. All his sisters live right here among us. Where did he learn all these things? (Matthew 13:55-56).

Some say that these children were Joseph's from a previous marriage, but there is no mention of them in the Nativity narratives in Matthew 1–2 and Luke 1–2 or anywhere else in Scripture. It is safe to assume that Mary and Joseph were a typical first-century young couple who married, started a life together, and had a minimum of seven children—Jesus, four other sons, and at least two daughters (the Bible says "sisters," so obviously more than one)—before Joseph died. He most definitely could have fathered six children before Jesus was 12 and stayed behind in Jerusalem at Passover (Luke 2:41-51).

Some believe that Luke 2:34-35 might hint that Joseph would not be around to see Jesus' ministry. Here, a man by the name of Simeon prophesies over baby Jesus:

> Then Simeon blessed them, and he said to Mary, the baby's mother, "This child is destined to cause many in Israel to fall, and many others to rise. He has been sent as a sign from God, but many will oppose him. As a result, the deepest thoughts of many hearts will be revealed. And a sword will pierce your very soul."

When Mary's days of purification following the birth of Jesus were finished, she and Joseph took Him to the temple as the law required. Simeon was there: "He was righteous and devout and was eagerly waiting for the Messiah" (Luke 2:25). Simeon knew the ancient prophecies and he was looking for this to happen. When he saw the baby in Mary's arms, the Holy Spirit was upon him, and he knew that the baby was the long-awaited

Messiah. When the Bible says that the Holy Spirit was upon Simeon, that basically means everything inside of him was firing at once, telling him, "That's Him! He is the Messiah!" There was no doubt in Simeon's mind. And when he prophesied over Jesus, he spoke to Mary, *not* to Mary and Joseph together. Perhaps this was a clue that Joseph would not be around to see the ministry of Jesus and His crucifixion. We don't know.

Nor do we know how long Joseph lived, but we do know God used this simple carpenter to help fulfill His plans for mankind. He was a good, devoted, dependable, and righteous man who worked hard to provide for and protect his family and lead them in the ways of God. We know he must have been a good leader for his family because two of Jesus' brothers, James and Jude, became early church leaders. They would have learned much from watching their father.

Joseph was a selfless, humble man, full of integrity and inner strength. He never spoke one word in the biblical accounts of the birth of Jesus. In church Christmas pageants, in Nativity sets, and on greeting cards, he's relegated to standing behind Mary, but he was the leader of that home. He led Mary and Jesus and their entire family in the faith. He was a nobody by the world's standards, but he was the man whom God entrusted to raise His Son.

Today, God still entrusts nobodies to fulfill His plans. We don't have to be popular or celebrated. We just have to be willing, faithful, and obedient, like Joseph.

FOUR

Looking at God's Plan

WHY DID YOU SEEK ME? DID YOU NOT KNOW THAT I MUST
BE ABOUT MY FATHER'S BUSINESS? (LUKE 2:49 NKJV).

Christmas is the only time of the year when we can walk into a department store or restaurant and hear Christmas carols pumped throughout. They're playing the songs of Jesus' birth! The very reason we give gifts at Christmas is because God gave the world the greatest gift ever inside those stable walls: the gift of His Son Jesus.

> This is how God loved the world: He gave his one and only Son, so that everyone who believes in him will not perish but have eternal life (John 3:16).
>
> Thank God for this gift too wonderful for words! (2 Corinthians 9:15).
>
> The free gift of God is eternal life through Christ Jesus our Lord (Romans 6:23).

In today's culture, the Nativity narrative as described

by Matthew and Luke, which focuses on Christ and God's gift of salvation, has largely been replaced by the full-blown business of Christmas. There are Christmas movies and music, parties and presents, decorations and dinners, trees and trimmings, and stage shows and sweaters. Yet during the crush and chaos of the season, there is something deep in our hearts that wants to slow down and return to the joy and hope of the Nativity. As we step into a local business and hear "Hark! The Herald Angels Sing," something inside takes us back to the beauty of the manger.

When we look at the birth of Christ, we must acknowledge God's plan in sending the Savior. The birth of Jesus wasn't an accident. It was a life-changing event that had lovingly been planned by God the Father. But why would Jesus even want to leave the perfection and splendor of heaven for this earthly world? When He was 12 years old, Jesus went to Jerusalem to observe Passover with His parents. On the way home, Joseph and Mary realized that Jesus was not within the company they were traveling with. They hurried back to Jerusalem, where three long days later, they found Him in the temple, listening to teachers and asking questions. When Mary pointed out that they had been anxiously looking for Him, Jesus said, "Why did you seek Me?

Did you not know that I must be about My Father's business?" (Luke 2:49 NKJV).

God had an appointed time for Jesus to come to earth—"when the right time came, God sent his Son, born of a woman" (Galatians 4:4)—and His mission of being "about my Father's business" would begin inside that stable in Bethlehem. He came from the glories of heaven to take on human flesh so He could live in our world and save sinners from eternity without Him. That was His Father's business. When speaking of Zacchaeus, the tax collector, Jesus said, "The Son of Man came to seek and save those who are lost" (Luke 19:10). "'The time promised by God has come at last!' he announced. 'The Kingdom of God is near! Repent of your sins and believe the Good News!'" (Mark 1:15).

Jesus' ministry of being about His Father's business of seeking and saving the lost began in the stable in Bethlehem, and throughout His life, Jesus never lost sight of that mission. In His teachings, He was about His Father's business. In His relationships, He was about His Father's business. In His interactions with lepers, prostitutes, tax collectors, the blind, the deaf, the mute, Gentiles, Roman soldiers, and religious leaders, He was about His Father's business. And in His torture and death on the cross, Jesus was still about His Father's business.

Jesus' first recorded words in the Bible at the age of 12 are about the Father; even at that young age, His life was engaged in His Father's business. Jesus' relationship with His Father was the most important in His life; it was so obvious that He asked His parents, "Why did you seek Me?" As if to say, "Surely you should know where I would be!" Think about that question in your own life. Throughout the Bible, even in the story of the Nativity, we see people like the shepherds and the magi, who sought out Jesus. But there were others, like King Herod, who only pretended to seek Him. We'll look more into those who set their minds on seeking Him, but what about you? Do you seek Him? If you haven't, why not seek Him now? The Bible urges us,

> Seek the LORD while you can find him.
> Call on him now while he is near
> (Isaiah 55:6).

THE BIRTH OF JESUS BEFORE THE BIRTH OF JESUS

The Bible is the only religious text in the world that includes prophecies that have been fulfilled with 100 percent accuracy. God, because of His great love for us, tells us beforehand what will happen in the future. He doesn't do that to scare us, but to prepare us. He wants us to keep our eyes looking upward to Him. He knew we needed a Savior, and long before Christ came to earth, God gave us clues about His birth so people would recognize Him when He arrived.

After Adam and Eve rebelled against God and fell into sin in the garden of Eden, God said this:

> I will cause hostility between you and the woman,
>   and between your offspring and her offspring.
> He will strike your head,
>   and you will strike his heel
> (Genesis 3:15).

Approximately 1,500 years before Christ was born, God revealed that this offspring would crush the head of the serpent who had caused all of mankind to fall into sin. A Savior was coming! This offspring didn't point to just any man but to Jesus, the only One worthy to crush the head of Satan.

Isaiah 7:14, which was written more than 700 years before Christ was born, says, "The Lord himself will give you the sign. Look! The virgin will conceive a child! She will give birth to a son and will call him Immanuel (which means 'God is with us')."

Isaiah 9:6 says,

> A child is born to us,
>   a son is given to us.
> The government will rest on his shoulders.

> And he will be called:
> Wonderful Counselor, Mighty God,
>   Everlasting Father, Prince of Peace.

In Micah 5:2 is another prophecy about Christ's birth, which was written approximately 800 years before Jesus was born:

> You, O Bethlehem Ephrathah,
>   are only a small village among all the peo-
> ple of Judah.
> Yet a ruler of Israel,
>   whose origins are in the distant past,
>   will come from you on my behalf.

This is one the most specific prophecies of the Messiah in the Bible. It clearly designates this town as Bethlehem *Ephrathah* (located about five miles south of Jerusalem), so it is not confused with Bethlehem of Zebulun (also called Bethlehem of Galilee) mentioned in Joshua 19:15, which was located northwest of Nazareth. That's how specific the Bible is when it comes to prophecy! God wanted to make sure that everyone knew Jesus would be born in Bethlehem Ephrathah and not the other Bethlehem. This prophecy is remarkable because Bethlehem means "house of bread," and Jesus called Himself "the true bread...who comes down from heaven and gives life to the world" and "the bread of life" (John 6:33, 35).

The Bread that we need to sustain us was born in that Bethlehem manger.

Not only does the prophecy say Jesus would be born in Bethlehem, but also, He will one day come to us on God's behalf and rule over Israel. Micah 5:2 says this ruler's origins are "in the distant past," meaning, in Hebrew, "that which is before, beginning, aforetime." God had already planned from before time that at a specific time Jesus would come from eternity to Bethlehem Ephrathah. The birth of Jesus was not an afterthought or plan B, but God's plan A from the very beginning, and is proof that God keeps His promises to us.

BREAD AND FRUITFULNESS

The first mention of Bethlehem Ephrath in Scripture is in Genesis 48:7. There, we read that Jacob's beloved wife Rachel died as they were traveling to Bethlehem, and "with great sorrow," he "buried her there beside the road to Ephrath." Bethlehem was a small, walled town built into a hillside. Ephrath or Ephrathah means "place of fruitfulness" and hints to an agricultural region that includes vineyards. Christ-followers are known by their fruit (Matthew 7:15-20) and the fruit of the Spirit (Galatians 5:22-23). Jesus said, "When you produce much fruit, you are my true disciples" (John 15:8).

The Bible's account of Ruth and Boaz, found in the

book of Ruth, further indicates the fruitful land found in Bethlehem. Ruth's life was radically changed when she and her mother-in-law left Moab for Bethlehem. It was in a valley east of Bethlehem where Ruth gleaned the fields and met Boaz, her kinsman-redeemer, whom she would marry. Ruth was the great-grandmother of King David and is listed in the genealogy of Jesus (Matthew 1:5). Bethlehem is also the birthplace of King David. It is where he grew up as a shepherd and where Samuel anointed him as king (1 Samuel 16:4-13).

God made certain that even the name Bethlehem Ephrathah (bread and fruitfulness) would point people to Jesus and salvation. Bethlehem had already existed for centuries before Joseph and Mary made their way through the crowded streets for Emperor Augustus's census (Luke 2:1-5) in search of lodging.[7] They were observant Jews and familiar with the legacy of Bethlehem, the stories of Jacob and Rachel, of Ruth and Boaz, and of course, King David. But they had little inkling that they were about to play a part in the greatest legacy in all of history.

FIVE

Looking at Elizabeth and Zechariah

ZECHARIAH AND ELIZABETH WERE RIGHTEOUS IN GOD'S EYES (LUKE 1:6).

My husband and I were married for 12 years before our first daughter, Grace, was placed in my arms in China. The road of infertility can be a long one to travel, even in today's era of modern medicine. I can't imagine what it was like in first-century Israel, when the stigma that was attached to childlessness was great. To those who lived in that culture, childlessness was viewed as evidence of God's disfavor. The assumption was that surely there must be sin in the lives of the parents, especially the woman!

Mary's cousin Elizabeth was unable to conceive, and she and her husband Zechariah were both "very old" (Luke 1:7). It would have been legal for Zechariah to divorce Elizabeth and trade her out for a much younger wife who could give him a son. But Luke says that "Zechariah and Elizabeth were righteous in God's eyes, careful to obey all of the Lord's commandments and regulations" (Luke 1:6). A righteous man would not divorce his wife just because she was barren.

Zechariah was a priest in the temple, and Elizabeth had been the daughter of a priest from the line of Aaron. Imagine the tongues that were wagging when a priest and the descendant of a priest could not have children! What sort of sordid secret sin was in their lives? Zechariah was not like the many other priests at that time, who were proud and self-seeking. In Jesus' parable of the good Samaritan, when a man is attacked and robbed and left half-dead on the side of the road, a priest passes by on the other side, avoiding him. But Zechariah was not like that. He and Elizabeth could have lived in the elite part of Jerusalem with the other priests and their families, but they chose to live in the hilly region south of Jerusalem. Their faith wasn't for show; it was for real. Their aged bodies told them that they could not have a child, but despite the hopelessness they may have felt, that did not stop Zechariah from praying for one (Luke 1:13). After all, "with God nothing shall be impossible" (verse 37 KJV). Zechariah could have easily given up, but he kept taking his problem to God week after week, year after year, praying and waiting, praying and waiting.

One day, it was Zechariah's turn to minister before the golden altar of incense inside the Holy Place of the temple. Centuries earlier, King David had divided the priests into 24 courses, and the order of Abijah, Zechariah's order, was the eighth in line. During the entire year, each course would minister in the temple only two times, each occasion lasting for a week. With 24 courses of priests and nearly 1,000 priests in each course, you can see that ministering before the golden altar of incense was potentially a once-in-a-lifetime opportunity. But today was Zechariah's day. Boy, was it ever! He had been chosen by lot to enter the sanctuary and burn the incense.

Zechariah entered the Holy Place alone bearing the golden censer, which would spread the incense over the coals when he swung it back and forth. As the incense burnt, a cloud of fragrance arose from the altar as the prayers of the crowd outside the temple rose to heaven. In our mind's eye, we can see him swinging that censer of incense back and forth, back and forth. As he did so, an angel of the Lord appeared to him. Yes, another angelic visit, although this was actually the first of the angelic visits in the Nativity narratives. Gabriel appeared to Zechariah before he visited Mary, and Zechariah's reaction was the same as Mary's and Joseph's—he was afraid. This should be enough to tell us that angels aren't cute little pudgy cherubs like those portrayed in cartoons. A real angel's presence strikes fear in people.

GOD'S MESSAGE TO ZECHARIAH AND ELIZABETH

"Zechariah was shaken and overwhelmed with fear when he saw him. But the angel said, 'Don't be afraid, Zechariah! God has heard your prayer. Your wife, Elizabeth, will give you a son, and you are to name him John. You will have great joy and gladness, and many will rejoice at his birth'" (Luke 1:12-13).

Zechariah's years of praying for a child were being answered, and he and Elizabeth would be filled with joy and gladness! This should give hope to you as you continue to pray for whatever has been on your heart for many years—your child, your spouse or parent, your town or country, your church, your health, or whatever you've been praying for. God has heard your prayers. He has listened to every word and has caught every tear. When you think nothing is happening or God isn't listening, keep praying!

The angel went on to tell Zechariah that John would be a special child:

> He will be great in the eyes of the Lord. He must never touch wine or other alcoholic drinks. He will be filled with the Holy Spirit,

even before his birth. And he will turn many
Israelites to the Lord their God. He will be a
man with the spirit and power of Elijah. He
will prepare the people for the coming of the
Lord. He will turn the hearts of the fathers to
their children, and he will cause those who are
rebellious to accept the wisdom of the godly
(verses 15-17).

For 400 years, the Lord hadn't spoken to His people through any prophets. But He had still been moving on their behalf, and at the right time, He would set His plan of salvation into motion. That included using Zechariah and Elizabeth, whose son would be filled with the Holy Spirit even while he was in Elizabeth's womb! Zechariah must have been astonished at the angel's words. But there was more. Their son would turn the hearts of the Israelites to God.

But Gabriel still wasn't finished. God's word from hundreds of years earlier was coming to pass. Zechariah and Elizabeth were faithful Jews—they knew the prophecies that pointed to a coming Messiah. Just like he would do with Mary and Joseph, Gabriel quoted one of God's prophets, Malachi:

Look! I am sending my messenger, and he
will prepare the way before me...Look, I am

> sending you the prophet Elijah before the
> great and dreadful day of the LORD arrives.
> His preaching will turn the hearts of fathers
> to their children, and the hearts of children to
> their fathers (Malachi 3:1, 4:5-6).

This news is almost too much to grasp. Their son would grow up to be a man with the spirit and power of the great prophet Elijah and serve as the forerunner of the Messiah! Zechariah was surely trembling at Gabriel's words. Maybe at this point, Zechariah dropped the censer full of incense. Their baby boy would be the one whom not only Malachi, but also the prophet Isaiah (Isaiah 40:3-5), foretold.

Zechariah had been faithful to serve the Lord and to pray all these years, but at this moment, his faith falters, just as our own faith questions and doubts at certain times. His faith wavers and disbelief washes over him. He's well aware of how old he and Elizabeth are, and at the moment, he must have forgotten that Abraham and Sarah also had a child when they were very old. Zechariah said to the angel, "How can I be sure this will happen? I'm an old man now, and my wife is also well along in years" (Luke 1:18).

Gabriel took a moment to help this old-timer along in his faith and said, "I am Gabriel! I stand in the very presence of God. It was he who sent me to bring you this good news! But now, since you didn't believe what I said, you will be silent and unable to speak until the child is born. For my words will certainly be fulfilled at the proper time" (verses 19-20).

The angel Gabriel stands in the very presence of God. If he says he has a word from the Lord, it's solid truth! The punishment of being made mute may sound like a harsh rebuke to shaky faith, but this is actually a gracious response. Zechariah's silence would lead him to greater belief, and the sign for when his speech would return would be the birth of the baby. Gabriel's words would be fulfilled at "the proper time." God's Word is always fulfilled at the proper time in each of our lives.

Apparently Zechariah must have been hard-of-hearing because after the baby was born, friends were gesturing to him to inquire about the baby's name (verse 62). So for Zechariah to lose his voice must have been an additional challenge. But in the silence, his faith in God's promises became stronger, and his trust in the Lord grew deeper. The words in Ecclesiastes 3:7 that there is "a time to be quiet and a time to speak" must have rung like a bell each day in Zechariah's mind. And how many times did he consider the prophet Zechariah's words written 500 years earlier? "Be silent before the LORD, all humanity, for he is springing into action from his holy dwelling" (Zechariah 2:13). God was springing into action! He was doing something that, for centuries, the Jews had prayed for. He was sending the Messiah. The 400 years of silence were ending!

JOY AND GLADNESS

That week of service must have felt like eternity in some ways for Zechariah. Surely, when it was over, he ran through the streets and rushed home to Elizabeth. Because he couldn't talk, all he could do to communicate was clap, pound on the table, make expressions, and flail his arms. People may have thought he was crazy. Imagine Elizabeth's reaction, for she had spent decades with him. Like any wife, she would have peppered him with questions. "What is wrong with you, Zechariah? Why can't you speak?" We can suppose he found a writing tablet and, with nervous excitement, quickly scribbled down what had happened to him, with Elizabeth peering anxiously over his shoulder.

Think of Elizabeth staring at the words, letting them sink in before tears filled her eyes. "'How kind the Lord is!' she exclaimed. 'He has taken away my disgrace of having no children'" (verse 25). Zechariah couldn't talk, so they wouldn't have chattered away into the wee hours of the night, but they could dance together and cry, and they could worship the One true God, who was worthy to be praised. The One who alone could open the womb of an old woman had given this elderly, wizened couple reason to rejoice. They would have a son, and his name would be John, which means "the Lord is gracious." How very gracious God was to Zechariah and Elizabeth. They had simply prayed for a child, and God was giving them more than they could ever ask for or imagine—the forerunner to the Messiah! John would be filled with the Holy Spirit while he was in Elizabeth's womb.

Just like Zechariah and Elizabeth, we pray for certain things, but God doesn't necessarily answer according to what we have asked or deserve, but according to "the wealth of His grace and kindness toward us" (Ephesians 2:7), "to accomplish infinitely more than we might ask or think" (Ephesians 3:20). God is still in the business of doing the impossible, so don't think for a moment that He doesn't see you or has forgotten you.

Just as Gabriel said, when John was born, Zechariah's voice returned, and he used it to praise the Lord and prophesy over his newborn son.

> You, my little son,
>   will be called the prophet of the Most High,
>   because you will prepare the way for the Lord.
> You will tell his people how to find salvation
>   through forgiveness of their sins
>   (Luke 1:76-77).

The 400 years of silence ended with the angelic visitation to Zechariah and the birth of a new prophet, the baby in Elizabeth's arms. Jesus would one day say of John, "I tell you the truth, of all who have ever lived, none is greater than John the Baptist" (Matthew 11:11), and He called him "more than a prophet" (Luke 7:26).

Zechariah went on to say,

> Because of God's tender mercy,
>   the morning light from heaven is about to
> break upon us,
> to give light to those who sit in darkness and
> in the shadow of death,
>   and to guide us to the path of peace
>   (Luke 1:78-79).

The morning light from heaven, Jesus, was about to be born! God is faithful and true to carry out His word even when all seems silent. He never forgets His promises. He still gives light to those who sit in darkness and in the shadow of death. He still guides us to the path of peace.

Elizabeth's pregnancy, like that of Sarah in Genesis, was a miracle. It was something that only the God of the impossible could do! Zechariah and Elizabeth had continued to praise, trust, and obey God in the middle of their hopelessness, and God gave them infinitely more than they could have imagined.

God is the same yesterday, today, and forever. He still cares for all of us who praise, trust, and obey Him in our impossible situations. Take every matter to God in prayer, and keep waiting and watching for what He will do.

Following John's birth, Zechariah and Elizabeth aren't mentioned again in the Bible. We don't know if they lived to hear John preach in the wilderness, "Repent of your sins and turn to God, for the Kingdom of Heaven is near" (Matthew 3:2). What we do know is that they left a lasting legacy of faith in the God of the impossible.

SIX

Looking at the Manger

AT THAT TIME THE ROMAN EMPEROR, AUGUSTUS, DECREED
THAT A CENSUS SHOULD BE TAKEN THROUGHOUT
THE ROMAN EMPIRE. (THIS WAS THE FIRST CENSUS
TAKEN WHEN QUIRINIUS WAS GOVERNOR OF SYRIA.)
ALL RETURNED TO THEIR OWN ANCESTRAL TOWNS
TO REGISTER FOR THIS CENSUS (LUKE 2:1-3).

It is late on the fifth day when they reach Bethlehem. The town is already crowded from the many pilgrims traveling for the census, all of them clamoring for a place to stay. Joseph's nerves are on edge as he seeks lodging. His feet are blistered and sore and Mary is exhausted. The contractions started growing closer together hours ago, and she is nearing the end of her strength. Mary is jostled and bumped as Joseph inches his way through the congested street. The crush of the crowd pushes them forward at a pace that frightens Mary.

People are bustling outside the inn, and Joseph leaves her alone on the donkey as he presses his way to the door.

A beggar reaches for Joseph's arm, but someone pushes the old man out of the way. Joseph raps on the door and can hear commotion behind it. He knocks louder, and a harried man with a pale face opens the door.

"There is no room," he says, before Joseph can speak. Joseph peers around him and sees that the inn is so bloated with people that some are lying on the floor or curled up on the stairs. The innkeeper and Joseph stare at each other in clumsy silence before Joseph thanks him and turns to leave, shaking his head at Mary. Her face is stricken as she holds her stomach. Her water has broken, and it won't be long before the baby comes.

"You," the innkeeper says. Joseph turns to look at him. "You can stay there," the innkeeper says, pointing to his stable in the hillside. "My guests' animals are inside, but if you can find a space among them, you are welcome to it."

Joseph surveys the busy street and realizes there is no place for them to go. He looks at Mary and she nods; they have no other option. "Thank you. We'll take it," he tells the innkeeper.[8]

Why was Jesus born in a manger? To answer that, we have to ask why He was born in Bethlehem instead of Nazareth. The Roman Empire was growing so quickly that Caesar Augustus decided to take a census of everyone in the empire to make sure that all proper taxes were being collected. Basically the census came down to money, and to keep it flowing fast and furiously toward

Rome. The census would include Jews who weren't Roman citizens. All Jews who were descendants of King David were to report to their hometown of Bethlehem. The timing of Caesar's decree was when Mary was about to give birth to Jesus. Caesar must have been giddy with the thoughts of more money coming into his empire, but Proverbs 21:1 tells us, "The king's heart is like a stream of water directed by the Lord; he guides it wherever he pleases." Caesar was simply being used by God to fulfill His plan.

After Joseph and Mary traveled nearly 70 miles to get to Bethlehem for the census, they found that every bed in that normally sleepy village was taken. The couple who was about to give birth to the King of kings was turned away. Rejected. The innkeeper did not know what he was doing; he did not know Who he was turning away. There was no place for the One who would go and prepare a place for us in His Father's house (John 14:1-3). There was no vacancy for the One who vacated heaven for us (John 6:38). The only room available was inside a stable—whether that was a barnlike structure or an ancient cave in a hillside, we don't know. We do know Luke says that Mary "laid him in a manger" (Luke 2:7), and a manger is an animal's feeding trough. At that time, no one knew that "the hinge of history is on the door of a Bethlehem stable."[9] The simple circumstances of Jesus' birth are humbling. God's Son deserved only the best conditions for His birth, but to reach "the least of these" (Matthew 25:40), the outcasts, He chose to come in the most unassuming way possible.

God knew when Jesus would be born, and He knew there would be no room at the inn. A packed house was not unfortunate circumstances, but the very plan of God. There are no accidents with God; He directs everything to fulfill His plans and promises. It was God's plan and purpose for Jesus to enter the world in the meekest of places. How could "the least of these" relate to a Savior who was born into riches and honor and fame? God chose a humble place for the birth of His Son, and throughout His life, Jesus chose humility over prestige and the world's comforts.

NO ROOM FOR HIM, BUT PLENTY FOR YOU

When Joseph opens the stable door, the stench of hot, sweaty animals and manure assaults them. He hesitates for a moment—this is no place for a birth—but Mary groans, her face twisting in agony.

Joseph helps her off the donkey and holds an oil lamp the innkeeper has given them to guide Mary into the stable. The darkened barn frightens him; Mary might stumble and fall. The lamp he carries is barely enough light to read by let alone usher in the birth of the Christ child.

Sheep scatter throughout the stable as he leads Mary inside; a disgruntled cow stamps her foot and lifts her tail to urinate. Donkeys kick at the stable wall and bray, their breath coming out in puffy clouds of mist.

Joseph spots an empty space against the back wall that will have to serve as the birthing room. Mary can rest there. He helps her to the floor, and she leans her head against the earthen wall, her back aching from carrying the weight of the world in her womb. This is a dismal place for a woman no older than a child to give birth to a child. She hadn't imagined this pain when she told the angel she was the Lord's servant.

"May it be to me as you have said," she had told him.

She moans; the contractions are growing closer together now. Outside, the shadows grow still and deepen more as the agony of life awakens the night.[10]

Mary's cries would pierce the night inside that smelly, lantern-lit stable, but there were no royal attendants carrying expensive linens to come to her aid. Her only midwife would be her simple carpenter husband, and although the Gospel writers do not mention animals, I think we can suggest that a few tethered donkeys from the inn's houseguests and some sheep were attendants alongside Joseph. We can picture unseen angels gathered round inside that stable in which Mary pushed for what felt like an eternity. Then...the Eternal One was born. The birth of this little outcast would be Bethlehem's most enduring gift to the world.

There was no place for Him in the inn, just as there is no place for Him in many hearts. His life would begin with homelessness and end with homelessness. "Jesus replied, 'Foxes have dens to live in, and birds have nests, but the Son of Man has no place even to lay his head'" (Luke 9:58).

Oh, the crowds that must have been bustling in the streets of Bethlehem that day, all jostling for a place to stay for the census! As the town swelled with tax registrants, how many passed by the site of the birth without realizing that heaven had come down, just as the prophets foretold? The Son of God was here, but all in Bethlehem rushed by. The long-awaited Messiah lay just a few steps away, and they ignored Him. The world yawned, and it was God's plan. How many walked past that stable without even glancing at or nodding in the direction of a young, new mother holding her infant child? How many cursed at or pushed aside the shepherds as they ran through the streets, praising God for the birth of the Savior? No one had the time or the interest to take a moment to pause at that stable door and look upon His face. If they had, like the shepherds, they would have been changed—forever.

There was no room for the King of kings to lay His head, but He always makes room for you. Even in His Father's house in heaven, Jesus has made room for you (John 14:2). He has plenty of room for the tired, the lonely, the sick, the anxious, the oppressed, the outcast, and the hungry. The doors of Bethlehem were closed to Him, but He has flung open wide the doors of heaven to us. Jesus is the way and the truth and the life. There is no other way to the Father except through Him (John 14:6).

That aching hole in your heart can be filled with Jesus. That cry in your soul can be answered by Jesus. That gnawing in your spirit that says you are hungry and thirsty for so much more can be fulfilled by Jesus. The infant in the manger is all that we need to satisfy our hunger and thirst. Little did Joseph and Mary know that when they entered the town whose name means "house of bread" that humanity would never be hungry again.

SEVEN

Looking at the Shepherds

THE ANGEL REASSURED THEM. "DON'T BE AFRAID!" HE
SAID. "I BRING YOU GOOD NEWS THAT WILL BRING
GREAT JOY TO ALL PEOPLE. THE SAVIOR—YES, THE
MESSIAH, THE LORD—HAS BEEN BORN TODAY IN
BETHLEHEM, THE CITY OF DAVID!" (LUKE 2:10-11).

When my husband and I adopted each of our children, our friends threw each of them a welcome-home party, either at the airport or someone's home. All our family members and friends were invited to come and meet Gracie, Kate, and David as they each joined our family.

When a new prince or king is born, it is only the world's elite who receive invitations to celebrate the child: monarchs, dignitaries, scholars, even celebrities. When the King of kings was born, an invitation did not go out to the top echelon of society but to a few shepherds keeping their flocks by night. The very special honor to welcome the baby Jesus was extended to the least educated of men in a profession that was despised by everyone.

Shepherds were never invited to parties because they were on the bottom rung of the social ladder. For the most part, they were uneducated outcasts whose witness wasn't even admissible inside a court of law. Shepherds worked long hours, earned low wages, and spent many lonely days and nights making sure that their sheep didn't wander off and protecting them from bears or lions. Shepherds reeked of the flock and boasted layers of dirt on their skin. But on the positive side, they had good job security because no one else wanted to do their work! Why in the world would angels appear to *them* with the good news of great joy?

Neither Matthew nor Luke gives us the shepherds' names; we don't even know how many were out in the fields that evening, and we can only presume their shock and fear when, in the middle of their boredom, "suddenly, an angel of the Lord appeared among them, and the radiance of the Lord's glory surrounded them" (Luke 2:9).

God's glory surrounded the shepherds. I mentioned earlier there had been 400 years of silence since the Lord had spoken through any prophet to His people. That also meant there had been 400 years without anyone seeing His glory. But then suddenly, the glory of God shows up in magnificent brilliance and splendor to lowly shepherds! If you're keeping track, they not only heard a word from the Lord after 400 years of silence, but also *saw* His glory! What a kind, loving Father to give such beautiful gifts to those who have been kicked to the curb by society! God's glory brought them to their knees.

Luke 2 says "they were terrified." Of course they were! One moment, the skies and fields are dark. And then boom, an angel is among them and God's glory is radiating around them! Some of them probably fell backward; others might have raised their shepherd's staff as a weapon. And we can be sure there were some screamers and runners among them.

"But the angel reassured them. 'Don't be afraid!' he said. 'I bring you good news that will bring great joy to all people. The Savior—yes, the Messiah, the Lord—has been born today in Bethlehem, the city of David!'" (verses 10-11). The Savior has been born? Their minds must have whirled with the words Moses wrote about Adam and Eve's disobedience in the garden.

To the serpent, God said,

> I will put enmity
> between you and the woman,
> and between your seed and her Seed;
> He shall bruise your head,
> and you shall bruise His heel
> (Genesis 3:15 NKJV).

This child of whom Moses wrote was the Savior. Though Satan would bruise His heel, the Savior would bruise Satan's head! Satan's greatest nightmare was born at last. The shepherds, who had been cast aside and discarded by society, knew their need for a Savior. Just as you know you need a Savior as you face a diagnosis, death of a loved one, a broken relationship, an unplanned move, a prodigal child, job loss, addiction, or an unspoken heartache—"Don't be afraid! I bring you good news of great joy! The Savior has been born!" Not "a savior," but "the Savior" has been born for you and what you're facing. Don't be afraid.

At this point, the shepherds must have looked at one another with bewildered faces. "This angel is sharing with *us* good news for all the people?" They knew that no one respected shepherds enough for them to be the group that was "in the know" of what was happening. They couldn't believe their ears. The long-awaited Messiah was born, and an angel was telling *them* about it! Their minds were reeling. "And you will recognize him by this sign: You will find a baby wrapped snugly in strips of cloth, lying in a manger" (Luke 2:12). The sign was that the baby was in a manger. They knew all about mangers! They'd have no trouble at all finding the Savior!

But the blessing didn't stop there. "Suddenly, the angel was joined by a vast host of others—the armies of heaven—praising God and saying, 'Glory to God in highest heaven, and peace on earth to those with whom God is pleased'" (verses 13-14).

The word "vast" means "a multitude, a throng." We don't have a number for how many angels were there that night, but the sight of so many must have been overwhelming to see! God gave such a beautiful gift of His grace and goodness to these simple, hardworking men. When the multitude of angels returned to heaven, we can assume there was much shouting and jumping and running around the fields in excitement before the shepherds said, "Let's go to Bethlehem! Let's see this thing that has happened, which the Lord has told us about" (verse 15).

"They hurried to the village and found Mary and Joseph. And there was the baby, lying in the manger. After seeing him, the shepherds told everyone what had happened and what the angel had said to them about this child. All who heard the shepherds' story were astonished" (verses 16-18).

The outcasts of the field were the first to see the Messiah! Besides Joseph and Mary, it wasn't the faces of royalty but the dirty, sweaty faces of shepherds that He gazed upon. As they surrounded the newborn Savior in the manger, they may have recalled the words of David, a shepherd boy who likely watched over flocks in the very fields they worked and who became a king: "The LORD is my shepherd; I have all that I need" (Psalm 23:1).

"The shepherds went back to their flocks, glorifying and praising God for all they had heard and seen. It was just as the angel had told them" (Luke 2:20). As they went back to the fields that evening, the shepherds had all they needed from the Lord, the shepherd of their hearts. Their experience with Jesus led to glorifying and praising God the Father. When we experience Jesus and He touches our lives, we can't help but praise and glorify God!

Those shepherds became the first evangelists of the good news. All who heard the shepherds' stories were astonished, and we have to wonder: Were they astonished that the Messiah was finally here, or that it was lowly shepherds who were given favor from the Lord to know about it first? Despite whatever looks the shepherds received as they spread the good news of great joy for all men, for the rest of their lives, they would remember that peace on earth is for all those with whom God is pleased.

THE OUTCAST OF BETHLEHEM TOUCHES OUTCASTS

Shepherds were on the outside of society. They were looked down on and largely ignored. Joseph and Mary, two simple peasant people, were not afforded a place of comfort for Mary to have her baby. Had they arrived in Bethlehem with status or a prestigious name, room would have been made for them. But as nobodies, they were quickly cast aside.

✦ Jesus would be born an outcast, and only a true outcast can touch the lives of other outcasts like the poor. Jesus said, "The Spirit of the Lord is upon me, for he has anointed me to bring Good News to the poor" (Luke 4:18). His teaching humanized the poor and demonstrated God's love for them.

✦ Jesus looked on with love and compassion and was not afraid to touch outcasts who were shunned because of sickness and disease (Matthew 8:2-3; Mark 1:40-45; 3:10; Luke 4:40). Jesus was willing to touch the unclean, like lepers, and the lame, blind, deaf, and all who had been socially ostracized because of sickness or disease. He also didn't shrink back when He was touched by the afflicted (Luke 8:43-48).

In that culture, no one willingly touched an unclean person, and society demanded that they be hidden away. Jesus saw these outcasts and cared for them while everyone else was blind to their needs.

✦ Jesus honored women in a culture where they were cast aside and ignored. He not only spoke to women, but He did so tenderly and with respect, calling them "daughter" or "daughter of Abraham" (Luke 8:48; 13:16). I believe His great love for women originated with His Father in heaven ("for love comes from God," 1 John 4:7) as well as the love His earthly father Joseph demonstrated for Mary and Jesus' sisters. Inside their home, I wonder how often they recounted His birth and the shame that Mary endured in her village as a young, unmarried pregnant woman who had the outlandish story of being miraculously impregnated by the Spirit of God. Jesus had great respect for His mother. He loved her so much that as He was dying on the cross, He saw to it that John would take care of her (John 19:26-27).

Jesus valued and treated women with respect (Mark 5:34; Luke 7:44-50; John 4:4-27; 8:1-11). He even talked directly to women in public when other men would not (Luke 8:48; 13:12; John 4:27). In John 4, Jesus ended up alone with a Samaritan woman at a local well. Not only was He with an enemy Samaritan, *but also* a woman.

The world Jesus lived in discriminated against women. A man wasn't supposed to talk much with a woman, not even his wife, and talking to a woman in public was even more prohibited. This unnamed woman at the well knew the ancient prophecies about the coming Messiah, and when Jesus talked with her, He revealed himself as the Messiah that her people had been awaiting: She said to Him, "'I know the Messiah is coming—the one who is called Christ. When he comes, he will explain everything to us.' Then Jesus told her, 'I AM the Messiah!'" (John 4:25-26). In a time when women were looked down upon, Jesus not only revealed Himself as Messiah to a woman, but to a woman of ill repute. The woman in John 4 had been married five times and was now living with yet another man. In His goodness and kindness and out of His great love, Jesus did not look down on or judge her, but revealed Himself as Messiah to this outcast. That is who Jesus is! His genuine concern for this woman who felt abandoned, used, and unloved ended up in the conversion of many in Samaria (John 4:39-42).

✦ Jesus showed care and love to the poor, disabled, and those who were despised (Mark 1:40-45; 10:46-52; Luke 6:20; 17:11-19; 19:1-10). A wonderful account is told in Mark 7:31-37 of a deaf man who was brought to Jesus. The crowd begged Jesus to lay His hands on and heal him, but the Bible says that Jesus led the man away from the crowd. In a situation that could have been confusing for this deaf man (and which would have made him a spectacle to the crowd), Jesus led him away, giving him dignity. Jesus touched the deaf man's ears, which is a sign of intimacy and acceptance for the deaf, and He looked up to heaven. The deaf man's eyes would have followed His. For the deaf, this is nonverbal communication. Mark 7:34 says that Jesus sighed. My friend Scott Harris has been a member of the board of directors for Deaf Pathway Global for many years, and he says this about Jesus sighing: "All around the world, the sigh in sign language is a 'marker' of completion—Jesus knew how to communicate to the deaf person in a way that the deaf person would understand! Most deaf people see the man's healing *not* primarily about the physical change, but rather, that the man was brought into relationship with God and others; Jesus wanted the deaf man to know and experience God!"

Jesus then told the crowd not to tell others what had happened. Why? Maybe because it was the deaf person's story to tell! The deaf man could now hear and speak. What love and compassion Jesus demonstrated to this outcast! And He still treats all those who feel abandoned and tossed away with this same care and compassion.

✦ Jesus adored children and took time for them at a time when they were seen and not heard (Matthew

18:2-5; Luke 9:47-48; 18:15-16). He even said, "Beware that you don't look down on any of these little ones" (Matthew 18:10). Children were and are important to Jesus.

✦ Jesus tore down racial divides. Hatred between the Jews and Samaritans dated centuries earlier and was still prevalent when Jesus lived. The Jews looked upon Samaritans as outcasts and enemies, and the Samaritans likewise looked upon Jews as outcasts and enemies. Jesus told a teacher of the law that loving his neighbor was essential for receiving eternal life. The teacher asked who his neighbor was. Jesus then told a story about a bad guy beating and robbing and leaving for dead a man on the side of the road, and Jesus made a despised outcast—*a Samaritan*—the hero (Luke 10:25-37)!

✦ Still about His Father's business, in His final act of mercy on earth, while on the cross, Jesus blessed the thief next to Him, an outcast who would publicly die in shame for his crime. A criminal on another cross scoffed at Jesus and said, "So you're the Messiah, are you? Prove it by saving yourself—and us, too, while you're at it!" (Luke 23:39).

But the other criminal knew who Jesus was and said, "'We deserve to die for our crimes, but this man hasn't done anything wrong.' Then he said, 'Jesus, remember me when you come into your Kingdom.' And Jesus replied, 'I assure you, today you will be with me in paradise'" (verses 41-43).

Only the outcast of Bethlehem could touch outcasts with His love and mercy and bring them to Himself, outcasts no more.

WERE SHEPHERDS TENDING FLOCKS IN DECEMBER?

Temple sacrifices ended in AD 70 with the destruction of the temple in Jerusalem. Those Jews who were followers of Christ did not participate in giving animal sacrifices because Jesus had been the sacrificial Lamb who took away their sins once and for all (Hebrews 10:11-12). Up until AD 70, animal sacrifices happened year-round, which suggests that the shepherds would indeed be out at night watching their flocks, despite the weather.

Bethlehem is about five miles southwest of Jerusalem in the hill country of Judah. In the region are fertile fields, orchards, and vineyards because the climate is mild and rainfall is plentiful. According to the New International Version Study Bible, "the flocks reserved for temple sacrifice were kept in the fields near Bethlehem throughout the year."[11] Unblemished lambs for sacrificial purposes were kept near Bethlehem even during the winter months. Although shepherds were looked down upon, their job was crucial to the Jews, who needed lambs to offer. Each year, thousands of male firstborn sheep without blemish would have been slaughtered.

Jews commonly kept their sheep in pastures from spring to October. Many believe that because the shepherds were still tending to their sheep in the fields, the angel's announcement to them must have been no later than October. This leads us to the question, Was Jesus born in December?

Most people agree that December 25 is far from likely the date of Jesus' birth. It is interesting to note that during the first and second centuries AD, there is no mention of anyone celebrating the birth of Christ. Origen, a theologian and biblical scholar of the early Greek church (185–254), said, "…of all the holy people in the Scriptures, no one is recorded to have kept a feast or held a great banquet on his birthday. It is only sinners (like Pharaoh and Herod) who make great rejoicings over the day on which they were born into this world below."[12] By the third century, many Christians were Gentiles and celebrating birthdays was rather commonplace. But even if people wanted to celebrate the birth of Jesus, they did not know what day He was born.

Matthew and Luke are the two Gospel narratives

that mention the birth of Christ, but they do not provide the date. Sextus Julius Africanus, a third-century Roman Christian historian, believed that Jesus was conceived on March 25, the day the angel Gabriel supposedly visited Mary. Thus, nine months later, on December 25, Jesus was born, and this became the date for celebrating His birth. Some people believed that choosing this date would weaken the common pagan celebrations that were observed on that day.

Based on historical and astronomical data, there are others who believe Jesus was born in other months or years. What we do know is that His birthday was not celebrated immediately. It took centuries, but by AD 336, Christians in Rome were celebrating Christ's birthday on December 25. It took several more centuries for the celebration of Christmas to spread throughout the Western world. Not until 1870 did Christmas become a federal holiday in America. Today, many people who are not Christians celebrate the feast of Christmas, but that doesn't mean they honor the birth of Jesus Christ and the message of the Nativity.

I love that there is a designated day set aside for the entire world to bow before the King of kings as the shepherds and wise men did. We don't know the exact day or month of Christ's birth, but does it matter, and would a different date change anything? We already know everything that we need to. The Christ of the cradle is the same Christ who dwells within all who love Him.

Every day is Christ's day if He is our Lord and Savior! And if you don't know Him, every day is an opportunity to kneel before Him as the shepherds did, open your heart to Him, and be born again in His name.

THE SAVIOR HAS BEEN BORN

"The Savior…has been born today in Bethlehem, the city of David!" (Luke 2:11). This Savior would save people from their sins (Matthew 1:21). Every wrong thought you have, Jesus saves you from that sin. Every arrogant word you speak, Jesus saves you from that sin. Every act of disobedience against God's Word, Jesus saves you from those sins. He came to save each one of us from sin and all that comes as a result: shame, guilt, anxiety, hopelessness, fear, and everything else that keeps us in bondage. He saves us from eternal death. The Bible says that today is the day of salvation (2 Corinthians 6:2). So why don't you say yes to Jesus as Lord of your life and let Him save you from imprisonment to the things that bind you? His peace is within reach for all who call on Him.

The angels said to the shepherds, "Glory to God in the highest, and on earth peace, good will toward men"

(Luke 2:14 KJV). Jesus is called "the Prince of Peace" (Isaiah 9:6), and He said, "Peace I leave with you; my peace I give to you. Not as the world gives do I give to you. Let not your hearts be troubled, neither let them be afraid" (John 14:27 ESV). The Savior came to give you peace.

Thomas Merton said, "If you are yourself at peace, then there is at least *some* peace in the world."[13] There can be peace in your home if the peace of Jesus is within you. Chaos and violence would end in the world if the peace of Jesus ruled within everyone on earth. Jesus said, "God blesses those who work for peace, for they will be called the children of God" (Matthew 5:9). God's true children are peacemakers, not chaos makers. I believe that because of what the shepherds heard from the angels and what they experienced inside the stable, they were peacemakers for the rest of their lives.

I believe that until their dying breath, the shepherds talked to broken people, the outcasts of society, and said, "The Savior has been born for you!" Just like He has been born for you.

EIGHT

Looking at the Magi

JESUS WAS BORN IN BETHLEHEM IN JUDEA, DURING THE REIGN OF KING HEROD. ABOUT THAT TIME SOME WISE MEN FROM EASTERN LANDS ARRIVED IN JERUSALEM, ASKING, "WHERE IS THE NEWBORN KING OF THE JEWS? WE SAW HIS STAR AS IT ROSE, AND WE HAVE COME TO WORSHIP HIM" (MATTHEW 2:1-2).

In 2020, Jupiter and Saturn appeared so close together in Earth's night sky that they appeared almost like a single object. Many were prompted to call the sight a "Christmas star," hearkening back to another magnificent celestial event—the star of Bethlehem.[14]

The account of the star of Bethlehem at the birth of Jesus occurs only in the book of Matthew. Throughout the book he wrote, Matthew highlights God's love for and mission to those who were not Jews—the Gentiles (1:5-6—Ruth was a Gentile included in the genealogy of Jesus; 4:15; 8:10-12; 15:21-27; 28:18-20), including the magi who traveled from Eastern lands by following a star to worship the newborn king of the Jews.

Skeptics doubt that a star could have caught the attention of and led anyone, let alone a group of magi or wise men (royal counselors or scholars, not kings, as the song suggests) to Jesus. They simply dismiss the story as legend. Also, astrology was looked down on by the prophets and religious establishment at that time. Scripture prohibits and mocks astrology (Deuteronomy 18:9-12; 1 Samuel 15:23; Jeremiah 8:2; 9:13; Isaiah 47:13-15). Matthew wrote for a mostly Jewish audience, so why would he invent such a story when the prophets wrote against astrology? Because God can use anything to draw people to Himself. Are you concerned for your child who does not know the Lord or for the prodigal who has been away for far too long? Begin praying that God will use anything to draw them to Himself. I often pray that God will speak to those I'm praying for in ways that he or she can understand.

That's exactly what God did here with these stargazers! He spoke to them in ways they understood by hanging a magnificent light in the skies above Bethlehem, and in doing so, called the Gentile magi to Jesus. That's incredible! God is still active and moving today and can reach your loved one.

WHAT WAS THAT STAR?

For centuries, the debate has continued about the star of Bethlehem. In 1977, science journalist Walter Sullivan wrote a story in *The New York Times* and suggested it could have been a comet, conjunction, nova, or simply myth. Clearly, no consensus opinion has emerged in the decades since, either.[15]

In the ancient world, people viewed comets as a sign of pending doom or an evil omen. So why would three royal scholars see a comet as a sign that the Savior had been born? It's also unlikely that it was a supernova—the explosive death of a star, which drastically increases its brightness for days, weeks, or months. Supernovae, or "guest stars" that suddenly appear and disappear, have been witnessed and recorded going back thousands of years. So if such an event had occurred, other cultures likely would have seen it and written about it.[16]

However, in the year 7 BC, Jupiter and Saturn had three conjunctions in the same constellation. If those three conjunctions occurred during a relatively brief period of time, it's easy to imagine that ancient astronomers—really, astrologers—would not only take note, but ascribe some meaning to the event. Just four years later, in the summer of 3 BC, an even more striking planetary encounter occurred. Jupiter and Venus lined up in an event that would have looked much like the Christmas star. Much closer to our own day, the close alignment of Jupiter and Saturn brought about the Great Conjunction of December 2020. The idea that a conjunction between bright planets could explain the star of Bethlehem isn't new. A note in the Annals of the Abbey of Worcester from AD 1285 points out an alignment of Jupiter and Saturn that happened at the time of Jesus' birth.[17]

All the above are answers from science, but of course, this could've simply been a glorious and brilliant star that God put in the night sky so that the magi could follow its magnificent light to Bethlehem! Matthew 2:9 says the star "guided" the magi to Bethlehem. "It went ahead of them and stopped over the place where the child was." The fact the star "guided" them *specifically* toward Bethlehem, then literally *stopped* above Jesus' house, indicates it wasn't a normal star, nor was it planets. Because the Bethlehem star's movements did not correspond to the way stars or planets move, the best explanation is that this "star" was not a star, but rather, a glorious light created uniquely for the purpose of directing the magi!

WHO WERE THE MAGI?

The Greek word *mágoi* in Matthew 2:1 is translated as "wise men" or "magi," a word originally meant in reference to a class of Persian wise men who were teachers, priests, seers, and interpreters of special signs, especially in connection with astrology. Further definitions include a "deceptive person" or "sorcerer."[18] The magi of Matthew 2 fit the first definition, as they were astronomers who followed His star from the East to worship "the king of the Jews" (verse 2). Magi were well educated; they were top-level scientists and scholars. They devoted precious time to studying and observing the heavenly lights. They had wealth and power, yet there was obviously something missing in each of their lives. When they saw the spectacular and supernatural star, it moved them out of their comfort zones and onto the backs of camels for the long journey to Bethlehem. A journey that long could have taken several weeks or months— with no map—just a gleaming star to guide them. If that star had stopped shining, they would have been lost, but it continued to shine and led them directly to the Christ child. If you're a Christian, think of the ways that the light of Jesus inside of you leads others to Him. If the light inside of you is hidden, those around you won't be able to see Him, so "let your light so shine before men" (Matthew 5:16 NKJV). The magi referred to the star as "his star" (Matthew 2:2). There was nothing normal about this star; it was sent by God for His Son.

According to many greeting cards and church Christmas pageants, there were supposedly three magi who traveled from the East following the great star. We can only assume Christmas pageants arrived at this number because the magi brought three gifts to Jesus: gold, frankincense, and myrrh. There could have been only two magi, or there could have been twelve, or maybe more. We simply don't know. However, in ancient times, royal counselors would not have traveled that far in a small group of only two or three. There could have been only two or three magi, but they would have had several men traveling with them for their safety and protection.

How did the magi know that the baby that had been born was King of the Jews, as they said? Being from the East, and the word *magi* being associated with a certain class of Persian wisemen, we can propose that they heard about the Messiah from Jews who lived in that area. Many Jews were still in Babylon (which later became Persia) after the Babylonian exile in the sixth century BC and did not return home to Israel. When these scholarly stargazers saw a star in the sky that they couldn't explain, they may have remembered what one of the Jews had spoken in the past about a star coming out of Jacob. The magi could have turned to the Hebrew Scriptures and read, "A star will rise from Jacob; a scepter will emerge from Israel" (Numbers 24:17). These men were constantly studying the movement of stars and planets and how they related to life on Earth. Imagine their excitement when they saw a star that could be connected to a scepter, a ceremonial staff used by kings and sovereigns! They were not followers of God, but they chose to believe His Word because the truth of it was shining in the sky above them! So they mounted their camels and made their way toward the star, stopping in Jerusalem to gather more information.

"Where is the newborn king of the Jews? We saw his star as it rose, and we have come to worship him" (Matthew 2:2). Again, in regard to how many magi there were, two or three foreign men asking this question in Jerusalem would not cause much of a stir (the idea of a Jewish king would have been laughable, and the magi would have been seen as kooks and easily disregarded). But a delegation of several foreign men ascending on Jerusalem and asking such questions would certainly set tongues wagging! That's the kind of news that would make its way all the way to Herod's palace.

A KING IN THE DARK

> King Herod was deeply disturbed when he heard this, as was everyone in Jerusalem. He called a meeting of the leading priests and teachers of religious law and asked, "Where is the Messiah supposed to be born?"
>
> "In Bethlehem in Judea," they said, "for this is what the prophet wrote:
>
> 'And you, O Bethlehem in the land of Judah,
>   are not least among the ruling cities of Judah,
> for a ruler will come from you
>   who will be the shepherd for my people Israel'"
>   (Matthew 2:3-6).

So Herod and his "scholars" knew from Scripture the answer to his question about the birthplace of the Messiah, but none of them took the time to travel to Bethlehem (a little more than five miles) to see if it was true that He had been born. They all believed the scripture pinpointing the location of Jesus' birth, but didn't believe it enough to make the trip there. That's head knowledge. They had no interest in heart knowledge. Thankfully, the magi had both.

The announcement that there was a new king was disturbing to Herod; he could only see this as a threat, and Herod did not respond well to threats. Judea prospered economically during King Herod's reign. He extended Israel's territory through conquest and built fortifications to defend the Roman frontiers. He was also a great builder, which earned him the title "the Great." The rebuilding and beautification of the temple in Jerusalem, restoring it to even greater splendor than in the time of Solomon, was King Herod's greatest accomplishment.[19]

But Herod was a cruel tyrant and murderous thug. He was jealous, paranoid, distrustful, and would destroy any potential opposition to his reign. He was so paranoid that he constantly feared there were conspiracies against him. He had his wife killed when he suspected she was involved in a plot to overthrow him. Three of his sons, another wife, and his mother-in-law were also murdered when they were suspected of conspiring against him. So you can imagine his reaction to the report that a new king has been born. Now Herod wants to learn what the magi know.

> Herod called for a private meeting with the wise men, and he learned from them the time when the star first appeared. Then he told them, "Go to Bethlehem and search carefully for the child. And when you find him, come back and tell me so that I can go and worship him, too!" (verses 7-8).

Herod claimed to want to worship the new king, but he sent the magi to look for Him. He did not go himself. First Chronicles 22:19 says, "Now seek the LORD your God with all your heart and soul." Herod's heart and soul were not seeking the newborn King. The magi were discerning enough to look to the ancient Scriptures and follow the signs in the sky, so perhaps the hair rose on the back of their necks when they heard these words and made them wonder if Herod had sinister plans in mind. The magi most certainly had heard of his murderous past. If a baby has been dubbed "King of the Jews," then Herod would eliminate that threat as well.

The Jews stayed in Jerusalem (how troubling it is that no one in the city was in awe of or wondering about the bright, glowing sign in the sky or remembering the ancient prophecy in Numbers 24:17—"a star will rise from Jacob; a scepter will emerge from Israel") while the Gentile foreigners headed to Bethlehem.

"And the star they had seen in the east guided them to Bethlehem. It went ahead of them and stopped over the place where the child was. When they saw the star, they were filled with joy!" (Matthew 2:9-10). His star penetrated the darkness and led the magi directly to Him, just as His light still leads unbelievers to Him today. If you really want to find Him, you will. "Whenever you seek him, you will find him" (2 Chronicles

15:2). The magi had followed the star and were filled with joy because they had found Jesus!

The magi did not travel to the manger. Some Bible translations say they went "into the house" where the young child was, and other translations say "the place." The point is that the star was not hanging above the stable. By the time the magi arrived, the Bible was no longer using the word *baby* to describe Jesus. Matthew 2:9 says he was a child.

This tells us King Herod had been left in the dark by the magi. Once he realized that his plan had been foiled, he sought another way to kill Jesus and sent soldiers to kill all the boys in and around Bethlehem who were two years old and under, based on the wise men's report of the star's first appearance (verse 16). The wise men said the star had appeared two years earlier, so Jesus could have possibly been as old as two when they found Him. By that time, Jesus was more than likely walking around and saying a few words.

THE TRUE TREASURE

"They entered the house and saw the child with his mother, Mary, and they bowed down and worshiped him. Then they opened their treasure chests and gave him gifts of gold, frankincense, and myrrh" (verse 11).

With their treasures in hand, the magi bowed down and *worshipped Him*, the Treasure of heaven. They did not bow down to them—Mary, Joseph, and Jesus. They had traveled all that way and over so many weeks or even months with one goal in mind: to find the King of the Jews and worship Him alone. As happened with the magi, His light still penetrates the darkness of our own lives and leads us on a journey to worship Him.

Gift-giving was important in that time, especially when approaching a royal leader or someone in his court. Frankincense, gold, and myrrh were precious and costly gifts, the very sort of gifts that one royal court would give to another. Also, a royal entourage never left for home without bearing gifts from the royal kingdom they had been visiting. The young King had nothing to offer the departing magi at that time, but His Father in heaven did. "When it was time to leave, they returned to their own country by another route, for God had warned them in a dream not to return to Herod" (verse 12). God led them away from Herod and his wrath.

In 4 BC at the age of 69, Herod died an excruciating death.[20] The dazzling and amazing star above Bethlehem was just a short five miles from Herod's palace, but he ignored it. He was so close to the Light but died in darkness.

The magi rode off into history without further word

written about them. They saw a sign of the coming King in the skies, gathered up precious treasures, and sought earnestly for Him. And when they found Him, they worshipped Him. Their lives are an example for our own search for the King of kings. How awesome that God chose those of the lowest profession, the shepherds, and those in an esteemed profession, wise and royal counselors, to look for Jesus and worship Him. The low and the mighty. The rich and the poor. God's kingdom is open to any and all who will seek Him with a pure heart.

NINE

Looking at the Right Time

WHEN THE RIGHT TIME CAME, GOD SENT HIS
SON, BORN OF A WOMAN (GALATIANS 4:4).

I have a friend who is a Bible teacher, and she recently went with her husband to one of his work-related dinners at the home of a "power couple" where they live. At one point, the hostess said, "I know who God is, but I'm unsure of who Jesus was."

Her husband, the host, immediately piped in, "He was a prophet. There have been many prophets." He then looked at my friend and said, "Isn't that right?"

She responded, "Jesus wasn't just *a* prophet, but *the* promised Messiah whom all the other prophets pointed to." Before the conversation could go any further, the home's fire alarm went off. The host and hostess did everything they had done in the past to turn it off, but nothing worked. It went off for so long that the fire department showed up at their home. By that time, the conversation about Jesus and who He is had long ended. We could certainly talk about the forces of darkness and how they had worked to disrupt this important conversation at this power couple's home, but let's go back to the original statement from the hostess of the party, who was unsure of who Jesus was. Let's look at who He was and the timing of His entrance onto the world scene in that little town of Bethlehem.

The Bible tells us that Jesus came at the "right time." Galatians 4:4 says, "When the right time came, God sent his Son, born of a woman." God knew the right time for Jesus to be born, just as He knows the right time to send help to us when we need it. In Isaiah 60:22, God makes a promise about Israel's future, but it's a promise that is true for all time. He says, "At the right time, I, the LORD, will make it happen." So what was the right time for Jesus to come to Earth, and what was so particular about the conditions that made them the ideal setting for His birth?

J. Warner Wallace is a retired cold-case homicide detective and bestselling author who lived much of his life as an atheist. When he began to use his skills as a detective and sift through the evidence from history about Christ, he came to understand how Jesus changed the world. In his book *Person of Interest,* Wallace investigates why Jesus came when He did. Below, I am extracting information from *Person of Interest,* which

I encourage you to read because Wallace's research is far more detailed than I will go into here.

A COMMON LANGUAGE

Had Jesus been born before 100 BC, His message would not have been effectively communicated because there would not have been a widely shared language and letters. However, when Jesus was born, the Roman Empire had adopted the Etruscan-modified Greek alphabet and embraced Koine Greek as a common language.[21] This shared language allowed missionaries like Paul to travel to other countries and tell people about Jesus without needing an interpreter.

AN ENLARGED AND UNIFIED EMPIRE

If Jesus had appeared before 27 BC, His life and message would have been confined to the obscure language and government of the Jewish region in Israel, but "the growth of the Roman Empire would soon change that." By 27 BC, a Roman statesman and military leader named Gaius Octavius became the first emperor of Rome, assuming the title of Augustus Caesar. He dramatically enlarged the empire, capturing Egypt and regions around the Mediterranean. Most of this area became unified under the same economic, military, and linguistic systems. Had Jesus arrived on the scene prior to 27 BC, His impact on the "known world" would have been much smaller and more difficult to advance.[22]

A WINDOW OF PEACE

Prior to Augustus Caesar, peace was rare among ancient warring nations. "The history of antiquity is cluttered with power struggles and tales of bloodshed." That changed under Augustus Caesar. The Roman Empire unified much of the Western world, bringing the entire Mediterranean region under common rule. Many of those ancient warring groups were now under the same shared submission to Rome. A time of Roman peace began, lasting from 27 BC to AD 180 and allowed Jews, living in cities like Jerusalem, to retain their culture and customs (so long as residents paid a tax known as the *fiscus Judaicus* and obeyed the Roman laws). "This small window of Roman peace provided the perfect setting for the teaching and ministry of Jesus of Nazareth."[23]

A HIGHWAY SYSTEM TO TRAVEL

As the Roman Empire grew militarily, it needed roads. Lots of them. The Romans would build relatively straight roads to make the movement of military equipment easier, which necessitated the advanced engineering of bridges, tunnels, viaducts, etc. At an estimated nearly 250,000 miles, spanning the empire from Britain to Syria, these roads became a symbol of Rome's power. As I mentioned earlier, after the book of Malachi ended the Old Testament, there were 400 years of silence. God may not have been speaking through His prophets anymore, but that didn't mean He wasn't at work. He was setting the scene for the arrival of Jesus. By 100 BC, the stage was set for the peacetime expansion of the Roman highway system that was built and enabled Jesus and His followers to share His message and ministry far and wide.[24]

A COMMUNICATIONS SYSTEM

Until the invention of postal services, for much of ancient history, the only way to communicate a message was face to face or hand to hand. There were some ancient empires that had a postal service of sorts as early as 2000 BC. China, India, and Greece had various forms of a limited, regional postal system. If Jesus had appeared during the period of history in which any of these empires reigned (from 2000 BC to 30 BC), none of these systems would have benefited Him or His followers beyond the limited regions each nation occupied.

By comparison, Augustus Caesar created a service from 30 to 25 BC that became the most advanced system on the planet. It did more than deliver messages; it also transported officials and tax revenues from distant provinces to Rome. Forts and stations were positioned about one day's ride apart. By the time Jesus appeared on the scene, the Roman Empire was ready to transmit His message. But more importantly, people's attitudes toward religion would allow the teachings of Jesus to take root.[25]

A TIME OF RELIGIOUS TOLERANCE

In ancient history, conquered nations were usually forced to reject the gods they worshipped and adapt to the gods of the victors. The Roman Empire was another story. With each conquest, the Romans annexed another culture along with its languages, traditions, and gods, and those annexed regions were encouraged to continue worshipping their own gods. All the Romans expected in return was for the annexed groups to submit to Roman authority and to make offerings (however nominal) to the Roman gods. The Romans allowed the Jews to coexist among the conquered people groups, even though they did not worship the Roman gods. "Rome *tolerated* Judaism, even if it didn't *trust* it."

Jesus was born at this point in human history, when the Roman Empire embraced a version of religious tolerance unique to the history of the ancient world, providing a 30-year window of opportunity for Christianity to take root. This window allowed Jesus to preach a message His followers could communicate to the world. Wallace states, "Even *before* the arrival of Jesus of Nazareth, it ought to have been apparent to any careful student of history that events within the Roman empire were aligning for *someone* special to arrive, and for *something* special to happen."[26]

A PROPHETIC FUSE WAS BURNING

Jesus's birth at that point in history was the result of what Wallace calls a "prophetic fuse" that had been burning for centuries. Scripture revealed the future arrival of Jesus through the gradual revelations of the Jewish prophets who, over time, offered more and more details necessary to recognize Him. Had Jesus come earlier, few would have identified Him given the information they had.[27] But by the time the Jewish prophets had completed their description, it was simply a matter of waiting and watching for Him. The fullness of time had come. Jesus' birth in Bethlehem happened precisely at the right time for the gospel message to spread and change the world.

The time was perfect for God to send a Savior. "There has been born for you a Savior, who is Christ the Lord" (Luke 2:11 NASB). We can't save ourselves. Our sins have cut us off from God (Isaiah 59:2), which is the source of all our problems. When we are cut off from God, we feel spiritually empty and our lives are often filled with confusion, conflict, addictions, emptiness, worry, fear, anxiety, depression, shame, bitterness, regret, and chaos.

All the success, riches, power, and fame in the world will never satisfy that deep longing in your heart because you were made to know Jesus. And at just the right time, God sent His Son—the Savior who was born for you.

TEN

Looking at Jesus

I AM THE WAY, THE TRUTH, AND THE LIFE. NO ONE CAN COME TO THE FATHER EXCEPT THROUGH ME (JOHN 14:6).

He was born in an obscure village, a child of a peasant woman. He grew up in still another village, where He worked in a carpenter shop until He was 30. Then for three years He was an itinerant preacher.

He never wrote a book. He never held an office. He never had a family or owned a house. He didn't go to college. He never traveled more than 200 miles from the place He was born. He did none of the things one usually associates with greatness. He had no credentials but Himself.

He was only 33 when public opinion turned against Him. His friends deserted Him. He was turned over to His enemies and went through the mockery of a trial. He was nailed to a cross between two thieves. When He was dying, His executioners gambled for His clothing, the only property He had...on earth. When He was dead, He was laid in a borrowed grave through the pity of a friend.

Nineteen centuries have come and gone, and today He is the central figure of the human race, the leader of mankind's progress.

All the armies that ever marched, all the navies that ever sailed, all the parliaments that ever sat, all the kings that ever reigned, put together, have not affected the life of man on earth as much as that One Solitary Life.[28]

✦

The child born in the manger in Bethlehem divided the calendar from BC (before Christ) to AD (*anno Domini*, or the "year[s] of the Lord,"), or what many today refer to as the Common Era. Not just any man can split the calendar, but only the most important man of all, who changed human history—Jesus! When we consider deities and famous world or religious leaders from history—like Nero, Augustus Caesar, Alexander the Great, Mohammed, William the Conqueror, Napoleon Bonaparte, Gandhi, George Washington, Winston Churchill, Dalai Lama, Elizabeth I of England, Attila the Hun, the Buddha, Queen Victoria, Vladimir Lenin, Nelson Mandela, and countless others—we must remember none of them sparked the Common Era. Jesus did that. Everything changed the moment Immanuel—or "God with us"—was born inside that stable.

Immanuel doesn't mean "God far above us," but "God with us." Jesus was the image of the Father. Paul described Him as "being in the form of God" (Philippians 2:6 NKJV), using imagery that Jews and Gentiles of that time would understand. Ancient Roman authorities used a signet ring to press an emblem or a mark into a hot wax seal placed on letters or important documents. That wax seal had as much authority as the person who owned and wore the ring. According to Paul, Jesus, when He came to earth, was the exact representation of God. Although He was fully human, He did not give up any of His authority or deity. He was also fully God.

The Savior was born who would take away the sin of the world. The only way that Jesus could do that was by being fully God *and* fully human. When Jesus took on the form of man, He faced every sin and took on every heartache that man experiences. It is only a Savior who is fully human who can die. Because He was fully God, Jesus could live a sinless life and take on all our sins as He hung on the cross in our place. There have been no other gods in history who could do that except one. Within those stable walls, cradled in the arms of His mother, was that Savior.

Jesus redeemed us from our sins by dying on the cross in our place and provided a way for us to come to the Father. Jesus said, "I am the way, the truth, and the life. No one can come to the Father except through me" (John 14:6). He took all our sins on Himself and then gave us His righteousness, which makes it possible for us to be made just before God and have membership in His kingdom. If you're keeping track, Jesus has done everything for us. We dump all our sins on Him, and He makes us just before God.

Without Jesus, each one of us would die in our sins, eternally separated from God and eternity in heaven. Those who believe and put their faith in Jesus come to the realization that through Him, their past can be forgiven and completely wiped clean in the eyes of God. We are freed from the bondage of sin. When we make Jesus our Savior, death no longer has power over us. A friend who is a former trauma and cardiac critical care hospital chaplain shared with me that there was always a noticeable difference in response when a believer in Jesus died and when an unbeliever died. There was always peace for the believer because death does not have the final say.

But God's gracious love doesn't stop there. When we declare that Jesus is Lord and decide to make Him our Savior and to walk with Him for the rest of our lives, we are adopted by God into His family. As a child of God, we inherit all that Jesus inherits! (Romans 8:17).

All three of our children are adopted. Troy and I chose to adopt them. They are chosen, and they are ours.

The infant in the manger grew up and took our sins upon Himself, providing us a way to the Father, and the Father adopts each one of us, bringing us into His kingdom. We are chosen, and we are His.

✦ THE GREATEST GIFT

In this book, we have covered the joy and hope and truth of Christmas. In these final pages, I want to ask: Have you declared that Jesus is your Savior? I'm not asking if you believe He was a great man who lived an exemplary life, or if He was a prophet or a holy man worth emulating. I'm asking if you've declared Him as your Savior and Lord. Do you have a relationship with Him? If you don't know Jesus as your Savior but want to, I encourage you to pray this simple prayer:

> *Dear Jesus,*
>
> *Thank You for loving me so much that You came from heaven to earth for me. Thank You for salvation in Your name alone! I repent of my sins today and declare that You are Lord! I want You to be the Savior of my life and teach me Your ways. Your Word says that everyone who calls on the name of the Lord will be saved, so thank You for saving me today!*

If you prayed that from a sincere heart, you have received the greatest Christmas gift ever, and the Helper (John 15:26), the Holy Spirit, has now come to live within you. In time, you will learn how to sense His voice and feel His gentle nudges in your life as He guides you. If you do not belong to a church, please find one that unashamedly teaches the gospel of Jesus Christ. You will find friends there who will lead you deeper into the Word of God and into a more intimate relationship with Him.

Will growing as a Christian always be comfortable? No. But Jesus did not leave the magnificence of heaven to come make us comfortable. He was about His Father's business; He came to save us from our sins and make us holy, which isn't the four-letter word that our culture has turned it into. To be holy simply means to be set apart. Jesus was born in that manger so you could have life and have it in abundance in Him (John 10:10). Just like Mary, Joseph, Zechariah, Elizabeth, the shepherds, and the magi, you have a calling and a purpose in the kingdom of God! Jesus didn't come here from cradle to cross so we could simply go to church once a week. Just like Jesus, we need to be about our Father's business, serving Him daily and seeking His face. The shepherds and magi looked for Jesus, and when they looked upon His face, they were blessed. As you have looked for the

Christ child of Bethlehem in the pages of this book, I pray that His face will shine on you with blessings today.

> The LORD bless you and keep you; the LORD make his face shine on you and be gracious to you; the LORD turn his face toward you and give you peace (Numbers 6:24-26 NIV).

JOSEPH'S CHEST POUNDS WITH THE WONDER AND
MYSTERY OF IT ALL. HE COMES CLOSER, HOLDING
MARY IN HIS ARMS, AND TOGETHER THEY LOOK AT THIS
BABY...JESUS, WHO OPENS HIS MOUTH IN A YAWN.

THE SAVIOR IS SLEEPY.

AND SO, IN THAT LITTLE TOWN OF BETHLEHEM
SO LONG AGO, A SIMPLE PEASANT GIRL AND HER
CARPENTER HUSBAND QUIETLY SANG LULLABIES TO
THE KING OF KINGS AS HE DRIFTED OFF TO SLEEP.[29]

Notes

1. Donna VanLiere, *The Christmas Journey* (New York: St. Martin's Press, 2010), 3-7.

2. Megan Sauter, "The Betrothal of Mary and Joseph in the Bible," *Biblical Archaeology Society*, December 21, 2022, https://www.biblicalarchaeology.org/daily/biblical-topics/new-testament/mary-and-joseph-in-the-bible/.

3. Michael Jakes, "What Do We Know About Joseph, Jesus' Earthly Father?," *Bible Study Tools*, updated October 15, 2024, https://www.biblestudytools.com/bible-study/topical-studies/what-do-we-know-about-jesus-earthly-father-joseph.html.

4. VanLiere, *The Christmas Journey*, 17-22.

5. Jakes, "What Do We Know About Joseph, Jesus' Earthly Father?"

6. VanLiere, *The Christmas Journey*, 23-25.

7. In 2012, a 2,700-year-old bulla (a stamped piece of clay used to seal a document or container) bearing the name of Bethlehem was discovered in an archaeological dig in the City of David. This was the first archaeological evidence extending the history of Bethlehem to a First Temple Period Israelite city. Biblical Archaeology Society Staff, "History of Bethlehem Documented by First Temple Period Bulla from the City of David," *Biblical Archaeological Society*, July 16, 2019, https://www.biblicalarchaeology.org/daily/earliest-history-of-bethlehem-documented-by-first-temple-period-bulla-from-the-city-of-david/.

8. VanLiere, *The Christmas Journey*, 32-36.

9. Ralph W. Stockman, https://www.christianquotes.info/top-quotes /top-25-christian-quotes-about-christmas/.

10. VanLiere, *The Christmas Journey*, 37-45.

11. NIV LifeConnect Study Bible, gen. ed. Wayne Cordeiro (Grand Rapids, MI: Zondervan, 2016), 1221.

12. Origen, in Levit., Hom. VIII, in Migne P.G., XII, 495.

13. Thomas Merton, *Conjectures of a Guilty Bystander* (New York: Image Books, 1965), 198 (emphasis in original).

14. Jupiter and Saturn formed a "Great Conjunction" in 2020, the likes of which hadn't been seen in nearly 800 years. A conjunction is when two astronomical objects appear close to each other in the sky. The bodies involved can be the sun, moon, a planet, or star. Although the objects appear to be close, this is an illusion caused by perspective. During a conjunction, two planets are aligned in a straight line, so from our viewpoint, it looks like they meet in the sky. In reality, however, the two bodies are separated by vast distances. See Graham Jones, "What Is a Conjunction?," *timeanddate*, https://www.timeand date.com/astronomy/conjunction.html.

15. Eric Betz, "The Star of Bethlehem: Can science explain what it really was?," *Astronomy*, February 1, 2024, https://www.astro nomy.com/science/the-star-of-bethlehem-can-science-explain -what-it-was/

16. Betz, "The Star of Bethlehem: Can science explain what it really was?"

17. Betz, "The Star of Bethlehem: Can science explain what it really was?"

18. *Blue Letter Bible*, https://www.blueletterbible.org/lexicon/ g3097/niv/mgnt/0-1/.

19. "Who Was Herod?," *Bible Gateway Blog*, December 19, 2017, https://www.biblegateway.com/blog/2017/12/who-was-herod/.

20. "Researchers Diagnose Herod the Great," *ABC News*, January 24, 2002, https://abcnews.go.com/Technology/story?id=98107& page=1.

21. J. Warner Wallace, *Person of Interest* (Grand Rapids, MI: Zondervan Reflective, 2021), 13.

22. Wallace, *Person of Interest*, 14-15.

23. Wallace, *Person of Interest*, 15-16.

24. Wallace, *Person of Interest*, 17-18.

25. Wallace, *Person of Interest*, 19-20.

26. Wallace, *Person of Interest*, 20-22 (emphasis in original).

27. Wallace, *Person of Interest*, 74.

28. Dr. James Allan Francis, "One Solitary Life," *HolyBible.org*, https://www.holybible.org/resources/poems/ps.php?sid=47, originally published in *The Real Jesus and Other Sermons* (Philadelphia, PA: Judson Press, 1926).

29. VanLiere, *The Christmas Journey*, 56, 62.

Scripture Versions Used in This Book

An Invitation from Donna

To listen to the *Looking for Christmas* podcast, find out about Donna's book *Looking for God*, or learn more about Donna VanLiere, visit

WWW.DONNAVANLIERE.COM/LOOKING